ROADSIDE NEW JERSEY

NEW JERSEY

PETER GENOVESE

RUTGERS UNIVERSITY PRESS
NEW BRUNSWICK, NEW JERSEY

front matter illustrations: p. i, Route 33, Millstone
p. ii, Route 30, Mullica
title page, Route 40, Hamilton, Atlantic
County (sign) and Route 527, Warren (EggOmat)
p. v, Hoboken

Library of Congress Cataloging-in-Publication Data

Genovese, Peter, 1952–
    Roadside New Jersey / Peter Genovese.
      p.   cm.
    ISBN 0-8135-2061-4 (pbk.)
    1. Popular culture—New Jersey.   2. New Jersey—Social life and
customs.   3. New Jersey—Pictorial works. I. Title.
F140.G46   1994
917.4904'43—dc20   93-31172
                                           CIP

CONTENTS

Route 27, Linden

PREFACE

Atlantic City

 'm not sure when I came up with the idea for this book. Maybe it was when I saw the giant plaster chicken atop the farmer's market on Route 30, or the sign for Killer Coffee in the Pine Barrens, or those lonely roadside motels with the sputtering neon Welcome signs out front.

Or maybe it was when I finally opened my eyes and realized there was great color, variety, and character in the New Jersey landscape.

You're thinking: Wait a minute. Are we talking about the same state here? Strip-malled, traffic-jammed, smelly-refineries-on-the-Turnpike, bland, boring New Jersey?

Yes!

It took me years to realize there was another New Jersey out there, a New Jersey of homemade signs and amusing street names, of quirky storefronts and wacky business names, of architectural oddities and beautiful country churches, of roadside giants and strange lawn ornaments. Why it took me so long to realize this I don't know, since I've probably seen more of the state than anyone, having driven hundreds of thousands of miles in the past decade searching out offbeat people and places for my thrice-weekly newspaper column in *The Home News*.

I started reading billboards and signs instead of letting them go by as blurs, started to peer around the sides of buildings for murals and faded product names, started wondering about all those misspelled street signs and goofy business names—started, basically, to see New Jersey.

There are no postcard-pretty scenes here, no gently rolling hills and wide sandy beaches. This is New Jersey as I know it, New Jersey as most people see it—from the highway. All the photos except one were taken from inside my car, which explains some of the odd angles. Why did I do it that way? I'm not sure it was easier, but it sure was safer, and I wanted everything to be truly roadside; you don't have to pull into anyone's driveway or get out of your car and peer over bushes to see these sights. (Might as well turn that one mystery photo into a contest: the first person to write me care of Rutgers University Press and correctly identify the one I had to get out of my car to shoot will receive a free copy of this book from me.)

There are no long excursions into local history here, no discussion in the diner chapter of trends in Formica countertops and the evolution of salt and pepper shakers. I wanted the book to have a folksy, popular appeal. Maybe someone will come along and tell us what it all means in a book titled "Roadside Iconography" or some such thing, but that person won't be me.

The research, I am sad to say, took its toll—my trusty Volkswagen expired on Route 18 on the way to an interview, with 366,000 miles on the odometer. If there's anything remarkable about the photos—I shot close to five thousand—it's that I didn't expire while taking them. Most were shot along the side of the road. Many was the time I'd be sitting there trying to focus (I never used a tripod) and a truck would blast by. I'd wait for the car to stop shaking and try to focus again. Amazingly, I didn't get any traffic tickets. To all the local cops out there who saw me in violation of dozens of motor vehicle laws: Thank you.

Most outsiders—most New Jerseyans—regard the state as an industrialized, polluted, densely populated state with about as much appeal as a Turnpike rest stop at three in the morning. The New Jersey I want to show you is an endlessly fascinating place, a roadside-watcher's dream, with surprises along every major highway, down every country road.

Some of these sights will have disappeared by the time this book is pub-

Lafayette, Sussex County

lished. Signs are replaced by new ones, roadside motels are torn down for more strip malls, pirate ships and other irreplaceable treasures burn down or crumble away. One day someone will decide that the drive-in theater signs scattered around the state—the only reminder that New Jersey is the drive-in's birthplace—are not worth saving, and then even they will disappear.

But the great thing about the New Jersey landscape and the American roadside in general is that they are always changing, for better or worse. If this book makes you jump in your car and drive down a road never taken, if it makes you pick up a road map and find out where the heck Jobstown, Sea Breeze, and Oak Ridge are, then I've accomplished my purpose.

(One note: I've tried to preserve original or local names in the text and captions as much as possible, thus Whitehouse instead of Readington, Ancora instead of Winslow, Toms River instead of Dover, and so on.)

Route 54, Hammonton

Route 555, Vineland

ROADSIDE NEW JERSEY

Route 9, Somers Point

Lucy the Elephant, Margate. The official state travel guide calls Lucy "the only 3-story elephant in the world." I don't know of any two- or four-story ones, either.

Lucy from an unfamiliar perspective

THE KID WHO LIVES IN A WINDMILL

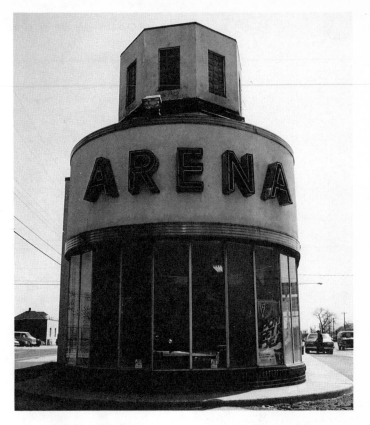

Car dealership, Route 30, Hammonton

There is no lady living in a shoe in New Jersey, as far as I know. But there is a kid who lives in a windmill. And a man who works in a castle.

"Definitely weird," says Billy Tonneson, standing shirtless in front of his peculiar home.

The windmill, located on Route 72 in Barnegat Township, looks abandoned and bereft.

Look closer. Clothes hang from a line stretched between two trees. A garden wraps around one side of the windmill. A treehouse is out back. Yes, somebody lives here.

The kid who lives in the windmill thinks it's neat, although like all boys he wishes his room were bigger. Billy's room is small, circular, and lacks a ceiling—a plastic sheet to keep out drafts covers the overhead space. All of this, naturally, tends to cramp a ten-year-old's decorating skill. But Billy

The windmill on Route 72 in Barnegat where Billy Tonneson lives

has managed to cram his toy planes and rockets, Teenage Mutant Ninja Turtle figures, Iron Maiden and other rock posters, Lego blocks, pewter unicorns, dragons, and other fantasy pieces, Nintendo cartridges, and a lizard cage—right now, minus the lizard—into the small, almost claustrophobic space.

"I tried to put up a poster, but I couldn't find any room," says Billy, who lives in the windmill with his mom, Julie, and her boyfriend, Bob Burnett.

"I tell people I live in a windmill, they don't believe me," Bob says.

They've lived here several years, moving from nearby Warren Grove. "We had to get out of my mother's place," Bob says. "An old lady used to live here; she was here quite a while. My mother knew the landlord."

There are several boarders—Bandit the guinea pig, Izzy the guinea piglet, Brat the cat, and Cracker the chicken, who lives in the backyard coop, located below Billy's treehouse.

"She's so fat," Billy says of Brat, who gets to her upstairs perch by leaping bravely across a space high above the stairs. "One of these days," Billy says, "she's going to fall."

Inside, the windmill looks like a house—a house, albeit, with six-sided rooms. The living room is immediately inside the front door; the floor slopes down into the kitchen and bathroom, part of an addition. Considering the windmill's age—it was built early this century—it is surprisingly low-maintenance. Considering its oddness, the windmill is little known.

"I don't recall reading anything about it," said a member of the local historic preservation commission.

"I've got quite a bit of Barnegat history, but I don't have anything on that," said local historian Fred Watts.

"All I know is that it really slows down traffic on that road," a township employee said. "I understand it has dirt floors."

No, it doesn't have dirt floors.

"We have to do the side again, the shingles," Bob says. "They're getting old. Other than that, it's a regular house."

They have well water, gas heat and stove, a garden ("My girlfriend's pride and joy," Bob says), and a television antenna, an unlikely sight atop the roof.

"Got to have that," Bob says. "No cable out here."

Asked how long he'll live in the windmill, he replies, "Probably a while. I like the area, I like living in it. I like everything about it."

A giant log would seem like a great place to live, but what is probably New Jersey's oddest structure is off-limits. In fact, even its owner, Mary Lou Krewson, can't touch it.

The log sits at the corner of Bay Avenue and Coral Street in Beach Haven. About twenty-five feet long, it has a barklike exterior and a

The log home in Beach Haven

splayed center door, which looks as if someone took several hacks out of it with a giant axe.

In the 1940s, it was a hot-dog stand several blocks away, along the bay. Moved to Bay Avenue in 1947, it served as a souvenir shop and surfboard shop. Mary Lou Krewson's father, A.J., bought the property in 1968. Then the Krewsons made a mistake, although they didn't know it at the time. They moved the log to their adjoining lot to make room for an addition to their house/bicycle repair business.

The Krewsons wanted to repair the log, but the local building inspector told them they couldn't do anything without a variance. The Krewsons have appeared before the zoning board several times without success. Their main opponent is Richard Greenhalgh, who owns and rents out the house immediately behind the log. Greenhalgh is a municipal court judge in River Vale.

What does Beach Haven think about the log? Opinion seems divided. Some consider it an eyesore; the log is in terrible shape. There are gaping holes in the back, and the whole structure seems in imminent danger of collapsing. A member of the Long Beach Island Preservation Society called it "unique" and worth saving, yet the receptionist at the Long Beach Island

Museum, a few blocks from the log, said she didn't want to hear any more about it.

When I told her I was going to write about the log, she smiled sweetly and said, "You should break your hand."

Lenny Duane is an unlikely-looking castle owner: bald-headed, tattooed, handlebar-moustached, with a Mickey Mouse cap, rose-tinted glasses, and a T-shirt with this message—Sons of God MC New Jersey.

Lenny, former policeman, former tattoo artist, current biker, assistant scoutmaster, and born-again Christian, works as a commercial artist in his castle on Route 57 in Mansfield, Warren County.

Lenny Duane's castle on Route 57 in Mansfield, Warren County

Maybe not the only castle in New Jersey, but the only one with this sign out front: Harley Parking Only. All Others Will Be Crushed.

Lenny's castle—at different times a gas station, pizza parlor, real estate office—boasts battlements, towers (made of cemented-over fifty-five-gallon drums), turrets (shingled peaks atop cinder blocks), even a stockade fence, which doesn't so much keep the infidels out as connect his studio-castle with the main house. The only thing missing is a moat.

"This thing of being a starving artist is not far from the truth," he says, smiling. "But the idea of living in your own castle . . ."

Part of the inspiration came from growing up in Warren County on, yes, Brass Castle Road. The rest came from his creative side; he has known since he was five that he wanted to be an artist. First, though, he became a police officer, in East Orange. He was an artist there, too; he did the department's composite sketches.

Then he started doing tattoos; his specialty was medieval-fantasy figures. His tattoo shop was in a castle, so he made up an appropriate business card—a pop-up castle, a fanciful version of his own, with flags fluttering and a face—his—at the window.

The card included these helpful hints for the new tattoo owner: "Avoid swimming, sun, and do not pick the scab. It will fall off naturally."

A tattoo artist working in a castle is a sure-fire story; Lenny was featured not only in tattoo magazines but biker magazines. He gave up tattooing, though, when he became a born-again Christian; he felt the two couldn't coexist. He says forsaking the easy money from tattooing strengthened his Christian witness.

He started the castle on his own, but quickly realized one thing: He was no castle builder. He enlisted the help of a mason. You can tell who did what: The smooth texture of the lower wall was done by the mason; the rough surface of the upper part was Lenny's doing.

"Some people have been driving by for so long, but they didn't notice it," Lenny says. "They stop in, ask, 'What did you do, just put this up?'"

He'd like to build a wall to connect the castle with his house, but wonders if the township would warm to that idea. His wife wants to turn the cluttered studio into a living room.

"I'm really flattered with the attention people give it," Lenny says. "I just want to be an artist—in my castle."

Route 40, Pilesgrove

Antique shop, Route 40, Mizpah

Atlantic City

Route 35, Aberdeen

Route 40, Egg Harbor

Route 46, Knowlton, Warren County

Route 36, Long Branch

Route 35, Old Bridge. The pirate ship, built in 1923, burned down in a suspicious fire in May 1993.

"After" shot of Route 35, Old Bridge, pirate ship.

One pirate ship remains, on Route 30 in Absecon

Probably the state's strangest-looking bar. Route 322, Weymouth

Route 537, Jobstown

BAD DOGS KEEP AWAY: ROADSIDE MESSAGES

Route 644, Pemberton

Up along Route 23 in Sussex County, one of the most picturesque stretches of road in New Jersey, Martin Little sells an important commodity to farmers and homeowners, some of whom drive all the way from the big city to get it.

Cow manure. But not just any cow manure. Rotten cow manure. The good stuff.

"It's fluffy, it's black . . . it's organic fertilizer," says Little, standing inside his dairy barn in blue overalls and green flannel shirt. "Compost."

Rotten cow manure as opposed to fresh cow manure. There is a difference.

Fresh cow manure is, well, just made. Rotten cow manure is manure that's dried out and aged. Little lets it sit on a hill and stew so that in the spring it's fluffy, black, and rich in organics.

"We stir it up in a bucket on the tractor," he explains. "It composts better when it's stirred up. That makes it rotten quicker."

You can buy rotten cow manure from Martin Little at his farm on Route 23 in Sussex County, or you can buy turkey manure—this sign (opposite, top) is in Atlantic County, or if you're lucky enough to spot a sign such as this one (opposite, bottom) on Route 47 in Cape May County, you can get your manure for free.

Something's rotten, it stinks, right? Not cow manure.

"The rotten stuff doesn't smell," Little says. "It's like picking up black dirt. Through the fermentation process . . . it turns into a black powder."

He puts up his bright orange sign—FOR SALE ROTTEN COW MANURE—on the side of his barn in the spring. And customers start dropping by. They pay about fifty cents a bushel for the fresh stuff, about fifteen dollars a half-ton bucket for the rotten stuff. Which one's cheaper? Even Little isn't sure, because the size of that "bushel" can change.

"If they shove two or three wheelbarrows in the back and give me two or three bucks, I'm happy," he says. "They put the money in the can by the firewood. I sell the rotten stuff by the truckload because I don't want people driving through the fields to get it."

He's sold the manure for years, but only in the last few has he advertised it with the bright orange sign.

"I put up more manure this year because we sold it all last year," he says.

Route 50, Laureldale, Atlantic County

Route 47, Cape May County

Asked how long he's been in the dairy business, he replies, "Always." His cows produce an average of 20,000 pounds—not gallons—a year. His number-one cow, Carol, gave 31,699 pounds last year. A cow's productive life is about eight years.

"I just lost the best cow I ever had," says Little. "She never made that much every year but every year she'd give 25,000 pounds."

His "gals" get fed a mixture that is 20 percent protein; his top producers get a 30 percent protein feed that costs four hundred dollars a ton.

"Don't make any sudden moves behind that red one there," Little said as he and helper Bob Clark fed the cows. "She's kind of ornery. Not to milk. If you go to do some veterinary work on her, she'll kill you."

One thing immediately catches the eye—shredded newspaper on the barn floor, used as bedding.

"Best thing I ever used," the farmer says. "Used to use straw."

The newspaper comes in handy when it comes time to do something city folks wouldn't ordinarily include in a farmer's job description—wiping cows' behinds. Little is particular about the newspaper he uses.

"The *Star-Ledger* and the [New York] *Daily News* seem to be the best for wiping them off," he says. "Some newspapers are very brittle. The *Middletown* [N.Y.] *Record* is very brittle. You can put your finger right through it."

There is one problem using newspaper for this task, however.

"Once in a while you see something, you got to stop and read it," Little says with a smile.

Before leaving, I asked him if he expected to have another good year in the rotten cow manure business. He said he did.

"If you don't, you just spread it back on the fields," he said. "It's not going to waste."

Route 9, Lakewood

On Route 579 in New Jersey's most beautiful county—Hunterdon—is a large sign on a wagon wheel.

THE FUNNY FARM, it says.

"One time, my brother-in-law Jim came down, we were killing a pig,"

Route 579, Pittstown

Ed Kuchman remarks. "My daughter was there with a couple of her friends. They asked us if they could have the eyes for show and tell. Weird."

If you think Kuchman's eight kids have a strange sense of humor, listen to him.

"We had a pig, bought it from my wife's brother, drove it back from Connecticut," he recalls. "Every time we'd stop, there'd be this stupid pig on the front seat. We got it home. It wandered over to the next door neighbor's and they kept it. We said, 'Thank God.' We said, 'Look, they stole our pig, let them keep it.'"

Kuchman, former mayor and police commissioner of Dover Township,

Route 9, West Creek

said that after twelve years there, he told his wife, Joyce, "Let's get the hell out of here."

They wanted a farm, and searched for one in New Jersey, Pennsylvania, Ohio—"all over the world," he said. One day they were driving back from eastern Pennsylvania. They got on Route 579 by accident, and noticed a For Sale sign on the farm outside Pittstown.

All the kids but one, their son Eben, who had just graduated from high school, welcomed the move.

"He said, 'You have to be crazy to live here,'" Kuchman recalls. "Now he has his own place [nearby] with a stream, two kids."

One of the first things the Kuchmans did was buy five sheep. One had a little lamb; the kids called it Lambert. Lambert wore a red bow, and got to be such a nuisance that when Jim stopped by one day to slaughter some pigs, Laurie, Kuchman's youngest daughter, tugged on his pants and said, "Uncle Jim, would you do mine first?"

"I still have sheep, ten live little ones," Kuchman says. "Do you know what I was going to put on the sign? Cute Cuddly Tasty Lambs."

"You have a sick sense of humor."

"I would have sold them," he says, laughing.

Life is good on the Funny Farm these days. All the kids have gone. The Kuchmans raise pigs and lambs, milk the cows. They have a horse, Sasha, and a donkey, Nick, adopted from the Grand Canyon for two hundred dollars and named after one of Kuchman's buddies. When he's not working, Kuchman plays golf on his very own golf course—several regulation-sized holes carved out of the fields.

"Golf's a nice game if you don't have to do it for five hours," he says. "Half an hour, I can take."

Any ground rules?

"If your ball lands in a fresh pile of manure, you can move it," he says. "If it's dry, you have to play it."

So goes life on the Funny Farm.

"It's been a fantastic part of my life," Kuchman says. "You'd come down that driveway and the kids would be jumping in the pond, having fun. That's what life is all about."

Wildwood

Route 33, Howell

Route 73, Cinnaminson

Route 70, Brick

Route 36, Middletown

Route 30, Berlin

Route 94, Vernon

Route 18, East Brunswick

Route 532, Tabernacle

Route 37, Toms River

INCLINED PLANE

ONE OF 23 INCLINED PLANES USED TO RAISE AND LOWER BOATS OF THE MORRIS CANAL, BUILT IN 1831. PHILLIPSBURG WAS THE WESTERN TERMINUS.

MORRIS CANAL
1824 – 1924
NATIONAL REGISTER LANDMARK
INCLINED PLANE
NO 9 WEST

ALIMONY IS LIKE PUMPING GAS INTO ANOTHER MANS CAR

BATTING CAGE

Route 9, Ocean View

Route 579, Port Warren

EAT PEANUTS WHILE YOU HAVE YOUR TEETH

Route 9, Marmora

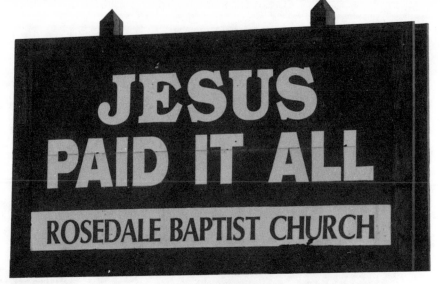

Route 561, Rosedale

Route 9, Howell

Route 555, Downstown

Route 34, Wall

Elizabeth

As if traffic wasn't enough to worry about . . . Fort Dix

Chimney Rock Road, Bridgewater

Fort Dix

Mansfield, Warren County

Route 322, Hamilton Township,
Atlantic County

Route 30, Ancora

Route 9, Dover

Route 36, Middletown

Route 40, Milepost 1–2

THE KING OF ROUTE 40

Route 40, Hamilton, Atlantic County

 ou smell the place before you see it. The aroma of smoked meat is in the air as you drive along Route 40 through Richland, Atlantic County. Where's it coming from? Over there—a sprawling, ramshackle open-air stand with a parking lot big enough for trucks, barbecue pits, and several signs hanging from the rafters:

WHEN THE KINGFISH COOKS, EVERYBODY EATS, says one. WE FOUND THE BEEF, says another. GO AHEAD MAKE MY DAY EAT A RIB, says a third.

Route 40—folksy, funky Route 40—is my favorite New Jersey road. It begins at Exit 1 of the New Jersey Turnpike, with farm stands, red barns, and the Friendly Tavern, and ends sixty-five miles later at the glittering spires of Atlantic City. In between are county fairgrounds, Cowtown, Placid Pine Lane, the Ca-Nook Motel, the Honey Wagon, Josephine Stapleton's milk jugs, Storybook Land, and many other roadside wonders. But on Route 40, only one man is King: The Kingfish.

The Kingfish's roadside ribs stand on Route 40, Richland

"You asked the best question, and I'm going to give you the answer," the Kingfish says. "You ask why I cook ribs and not something else. Now you know"—big smile—"black man can't cook no spaghetti. White man"—bigger smile—"can't barbecue no ribs. Black man can't cook no seafood, white man can't cook no collard greens and chitlins. Now what the hell I look like coming in here and cooking spaghetti and Italian sausage? You want me to break it down for you? I have to cook something white people can't cook. I'm not being funny. Write that down. I'm just being truthful."

The Kingfish's helpers

Milepost 4–5, eastbound side

Milepost 7–8, eastbound side

He looks at his barbecue pits, where one of his workers, known as the Iceman, was preparing ribs for the next day.

"Cleanliness, courtesy, and respect for the ladies," Kingfish says. "Other than that, we have fun. We have customers come here, say, 'f—— this' or 'f—— that.' You don't use that word here. We look dead at you. If you're not going to go, the state troopers will come get you, and we'll hold you until they come."

There's been little trouble at the Kingfish's place for the past twelve years. This is a man who doesn't want anyone to mess up his good thing. He knows how unpredictable life can be. Twelve years ago, Kingfish should have been a dead man.

"I got blown up by one of those truck tires," he says matter-of-factly.

Route 9, Lakewood

Fairy Tale Forest, Oak Ridge

*Off Route 295,
Gloucester County*

Peaceful Valley is located, appropriately enough, in God's Country, the name Robert Driver, Sr., gave to the section of Route 538 in South Harrison, Salem County. Driver's sign is located across the road from the Cabana's signs.

Belmar

Cabana's Peaceful Valley, Route 538,
South Harrison, Salem County

South Seaside Park

Outhouse next to an abandoned church, Jericho

Newark

Route 36, Middletown

Route 513, Middle Valley

Route 511, Ringwood

He was a truck driver then. "Just when I went to touch it, it blew out. Blew me the length of an eight-foot doorway. It busted me up. I spent two years on and off in four hospitals." He pulls up his shirt to show a long jagged scar on his back; it looks as if someone had taken a chainsaw to him. "I was fourteen inches from being dead or a vegetable. If the [tire] valve stem was fourteen inches lower, I would have been bending over and the tire would have hit me in the head."

He sued the tire manufacturer over the defective tire, and after a five-day jury trial, was awarded $1.8 million in damages, "payable tax-free," he notes, "within thirty days." "I'll tell you one thing," he says. "I like money—I don't love it—I like it, but it don't solve things. That $1.8 million wouldn't have saved me."

He was set for retirement, but knew he couldn't stay home all day. "I was getting on her nerves," he says of his wife, Christine. "I told her, 'I think I'll go down and sell some ribs.'"

Actually, the ribs were Christine's idea. Kingfish sold fish and produce at first, then started making ribs in his yard. Word spread. "It was, 'Where'd you get those ribs?' 'Kingfish.' 'Where's that?' There was no advertising, no radio shows, no TV."

Milepost 8–9, westbound side,
Richman's Ice Cream

Kingfish chose ribs, or maybe ribs chose him. He was born in West Virginia; his father was a farmer. "Cooking was the only thing we knew," he recalls. "We killed pigs, made meat all night long . . ."

He moved to the open lot, owned by Orlandini's Tile next door, setting up a fifty-five-gallon drum with wire strung across the top for a grill. He stood on a pallet to keep the snow off his feet. This was no summers-only operation. The Kingfish was open—still is—year-round.

"People saw me out there in the snow and said, 'Kingfish, you crazy.' I said, 'I was here before the snow was.'"

Now, what about those ribs?

"Everything's perfect," said Bernard Bennett of Vineland. "Any time she don't like cooking"—he looked at his girlfriend, Lisa Stone—"we come here."

Milepost 9–10, westbound side

"If you big," said Barry Stevenson of Woodstown, who fit in that category, "he may throw you an extra bone. I like that personal touch."

Besides the boys at Orlandini's, local characters include Santo Perugini, whom Kingfish calls "the mayor of Richland."

"He's got some good ribs," Santo says, grinning, "but I've got to go down to the dentist and get some teeth."

One tip: do not suggest to the Kingfish his ribs are like everyone else's.

"If you got no time, don't cook no ribs," he says. "Don't even try. Anybody can serve bones. If you ain't prepared to stand there three hours and watch them, don't even try. There ain't no shortcut to cooking ribs. Tomorrow I put these ribs"—they had been slow-cooking for several hours by this time—"through another process. I put them in pans, in some of my spicy water. Those ribs start popping, soften right up.

"If people can't wait," he adds, smiling, "they gotta leave. I will sell no ribs before its time."

"I can't stand the smell," jokes Robert Bruley, who works at Orlandini's. "It goes right through the warehouse. By the time it's one o'clock, you can't stand it anymore, you're starving."

"You put your wood in, it's got to be burnt down," Kingfish continues. "See that flame? It's steady. You got the natural flavor from the wood. Hickory, oak, or cherry, I prefer hickory any time. Ten seconds—if you can't hold your hand longer than ten seconds over the flame, it's too hot. You don't want to have that meat too high. You break down the tissues. It becomes too stringy. Looks pretty, but it tastes tough.

"You've got to spend time with your ribs, talk to them," he says later. "You know those ladies with flowers in their house, they talk to them? You got to talk to your ribs, too."

What makes his ribs good? His secret sauce, of course.

"You only get out what you put in. I don't use no cheap ingredients. You know what it would cost to buy a gallon of sauce from me? Fifteen dollars. Fifteen dollars, and you'll be smiling. I ain't cheating you."

The Kingfish sells ribs and chicken, collard greens and other vegetables. And don't forget his Brunswick stew. Stevenson calls it "killer stew."

"Oh, man, let me tell you something about that," Kingfish says. "Whole corn, green limas, peppers, onions, tomatoes, and the Kingfish's special sauce. That's the secret. Last week"—he took off his hat to show his

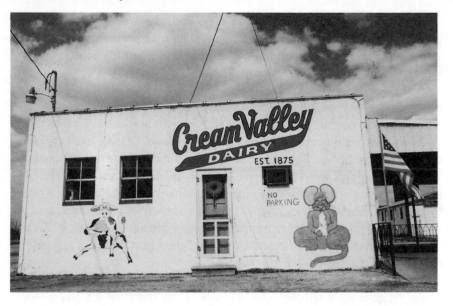

Milepost 11–12, westbound side, Woodstown

hair—"I was baldheaded." He often does this routine for customers when they ask about Brunswick stew.

"One thing it don't mend," Iceman says, "is a broken heart."

"When the doctor gives up on you, try some Brunswick stew," Kingfish adds.

That YOU NAME IT, WE COOK IT sign out front—he means it.

"Possum, raccoon . . . hunters come in, say, 'Kingfish, barbecue this for me,' and I do. But when I cook something [for sale], it's only USDA-approved. Make sure you put that in. I don't go out in the woods and cook something and sell it."

Everyone calls him Kingfish, but few know why.

"You watch the Amos 'n' Andy show? The one that talked a whole lot of bull—was Kingfish. He used to psych Andy. I used to talk so much, they started calling me Kingfish."

Many of his customers are on their way to or from Atlantic City. Redd Foxx's chauffeur made a ribs run once; a well-known gospel group stopped in their bus. Kingfish bought some of their tapes; they bought some of his ribs.

He lets you bring beer in, but whiskey is not allowed because "it has a tendency to make people crazy." In the summer, he puts tables out by the road; the tables at one end of the stand, on a dirt floor, comprise the King-fish's Lounge, open to all.

The Kingfish is open until dusk Saturdays and Sundays, but get there early. When he runs out of ribs—he won't say how much he cooks because he doesn't want his competition to know—that's it.

"Look at those babies, look at those babies," he says of a rack watched by the Iceman. "Cut them up."

Milepost 15, westbound side

Milepost 12–13, westbound side

Milepost 18–19, westbound side

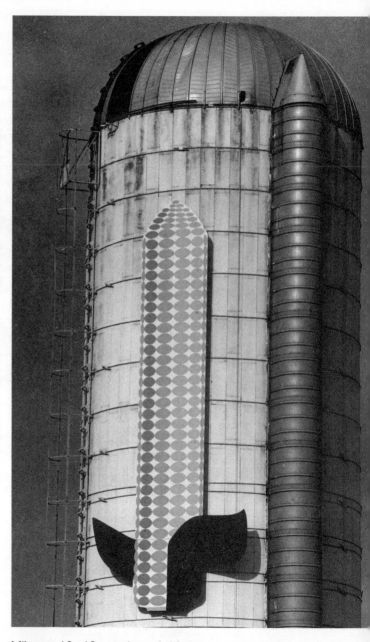

Milepost 18–19, westbound side

Milepost 20, westbound, Elmer

Milepost 21, eastbound side

Milepost 21, eastbound side

Milepost 24–25, eastbound side

Milepost 26–27, eastbound side

Milepost 28–29, eastbound side

Milepost 34, eastbound side, Landisville

Milepost 39–40, westbound side, outside Richland

Milepost 35–36, westbound side

Milepost 42, eastbound side

Milepost 43–44, eastbound side

Milepost 55–56, eastbound side

Milepost 59–60, westbound side, Pleasantville

Milepost 63–64, eastbound side

Westfield

EXCELLENT DINERS

Tick-Tock Diner, Route 3, Clifton

 rom the outside, it looks like its neighborhood: rundown, beat-up, seedy. The word DINER is spelled out in large letters above the entrance. A sign atop a grimy wall says Truck Stop Diner.

Inside?

Inside, it's bright, clean, and shiny, which will surprise the first-time visitor pulling up to that forbidding exterior.

Inside, it is lively, almost boisterous, as truckers on their way to Chicago, Miami, Seattle, Dallas, and elsewhere while away the minutes, the hours, the days. Owner Sam Kolokithas knows them all.

"He comes from Chicago, that's his wife," he says of a couple in the first booth.

Guys in the booth halfway down?

"They're from Minnesota," he says.

Guys all the way in back?

"Some from Chicago, some local guys."

"They do have a good cup of coffee," confirms Janet Sexauer, half of the truck-driving couple in the first booth. "It's hard to get a good cup of coffee between here and Chicago."

"Our cheesecake is famous," a proud Kolokithas says. "Everybody who eats here says they never eat cheesecake that good in the whole United States."

"I have never heard anyone talking about it in Chicago," Janet's husband, Mario Cittadino, says, smiling.

"I think this is the best little restaurant in New Jersey," puts in Ohio trucker Mike daCosta.

It certainly is one of the unlikeliest classic diners around. The Truck Stop Diner is located at the Jersey Truck Stop, on Truck 1–9 in Kearny.

The Truck Stop Diner in Kearny

Appearances can be deceiving: The Truck Stop Diner's exterior is forbidding, the interior charming.

You won't find tourists, businessmen, or young urban professionals in here. Truckers make up most of the traffic on Truck 1–9; motorists use Route 1–9 and the Pulaski Skyway, prohibited to trucks. And the Truck Stop Diner, located off the highway, is not the kind of place you happen upon accidentally.

It's a truckers' hangout; the atmosphere at night resembles a friendly neighborhood tavern, minus the liquor, of course. And it never closes, at least not between 5 A.M. Monday and 3 P.M. Saturday.

"In the morning, I usually have the corned beef and hash," Janet says. "It's like nothing I've ever had anywhere else. You can actually see meat in it."

In front of her this afternoon is a plate of chili and rice.

"I had chili and rice last night, too," she says, laughing. "I can't see why anyone would come in here and order a damn hamburger. That's ridiculous."

Truckers' Specials usually call to mind eggs, bacon, home fries, pancakes—all on the same plate. Or maybe fried chicken with mashed

Joe's Chadwick Diner, Route 35

potatoes. Or a big juicy steak with heaps of onion rings. At the Truck Stop Diner, the specials are apt to be leg of lamb and roast turkey, or oxtails and catfish. For dessert, some of Sam's famous cheesecake, or sweet potato pie. He makes all the baked goods himself.

"Truckers are coming in from all over the road and they are hungry," he says. "They cannot find food on their own."

For ten years, he worked in the nearby Skyway Diner. Four years ago, John Spanos, then the Truck Stop Diner's owner, retired, and Sam—"I wanted to get rich, get my own business"—bought the place. From what he heard, the diner was once located across from Madison Square Garden and was called the Arena Diner. About thirty years ago, it was relocated here. A plaque above the door shows the builder: Kullman Dining Car Co., Harrison. Sam changed the color of the booths from red to blue, put up curtains, added salads and specials.

"Lots of hours, lot of responsibilities," Sam says of his fourteen-hours-a-day, six-days-a-week schedule.

"We try not to eat a lot of fried things; here we eat a lot of vegetables," Janet says. "They use a lot of fresh vegetables. I know, because I see them coming in through the side door."

Bridgeton Grill, Bridgeton

Tonnele Avenue, Jersey City

"Where are the best places to eat between here and Chicago?" I ask the couple, who make runs between Chicago (they live in Calumet City, Illinois) and the East Coast once or twice a week.

"Snowshoe [Pennsylvania], Exit 22 [Route 80]," Mario says. "The Snowshoe Truck Stop. They've got good food there."

Janet mentions another Pennsylvania truck stop and grimaces. "Their coffee sucks," she says. "It's brown and lousy and other than that, I think someone dipped their socks in it."

"You can get some good Southern cooking there," Mario says of a Georgia truck stop. "Banana pudding—I've never tasted any better."

"Banana pudding—never tried that," I offer.

"You've got to get out of Yuppieville and try some real cooking," he says.

"There's a Union 76 up in Wisconsin, I want to say the western part of the state but it could be north of Milwaukee," Mike says. "It has all the Winchesters, all the rifles, up on the wall. They're in glass cases all over the restaurant. The owner has something written up on every one. You go in there, it gives you the history of the whole damn West."

Janet watches a pot-bellied trucker walk by.

"That's what we try to avoid—Dunlap's Disease," she says.

"Dunlap's Disease?"

"Yeah. It done lap over your belt."

"I eat McDonald's a lot," Mike says.

"Goddamn, can't you find something better to eat?" Mario asks.

Mike smiles. "Burger King?"

Janet and Mario stop at the diner whenever they make their overnight run between Chicago and the East Coast. They met here six years ago. She was in the bar out back with friends; he was passing through. She had been a receptionist, construction worker, waitress, warehouse worker. He had been riding trucks since he was ten years old, first in his dad's truck, now his own.

Chatham Wok Diner, Chatham

Deepwater, Salem County

"I thought he was the cutest thing I'd ever seen," Janet recalls. "He taught me everything. I was driving when I was eight months pregnant. Our honeymoon was a trip to New York in the truck. I wanted to hang paint buckets from the bumper. He wouldn't let me."

"I would have been the laughingstock of the industry," Mario says.

"We rebuilt an engine out there in the parking lot," Janet says. "Took three days. It was one of the first things we did together."

"I taught two wives and three girlfriends how to drive," Mike adds. "They all drive now and they're all damn good drivers."

All three—Mike, Janet, Mario—are independent drivers, and proud of it.

"This country was built on independence," Mario says. "If they ain't got that, they ain't got nothing."

"Your company drivers are more like sheep," Janet says. " 'Drive me to death, please.'" She smiles. "We're more like wolves."

But all truck drivers are alike in one respect, they agree.

"You have your finger on the pulse of America," Mario explains. "You hear all the gripes. We know more what the people want than the politicians."

It was dark out. We had been sitting there for three hours. Trucks rumbled across the parking lot, heading for Route 1 and the New Jersey Turnpike. I asked the three truckers the funniest thing that had ever happened to them on the road.

"I was going through Yellowstone," Mike says after some thought. "There was a herd of moose crossing the road. Have you ever seen a moose? They're big and they're mean. This [trucker] in front of me did something you should never do to a moose. He blew his air horn. That moose beat his truck up. He whacked the hell out of that truck. Bent the radiator. Kicked in the side. They had to call a tow truck. When they came to get him, that poor boy had crawled into his bunk. He was behind the mattress.

"I tell you," Mike says, laughing. "Don't blow your horn at a moose."

Maplewood

White Circle Diner, Bloomfield

White Diamond, Westfield

Route 511, West Milford

Red Tower, Plainfield

Plainfield

Route 9, Cedar Run

Hackensack

Route 33, East Windsor

Route 47, Rio Grande

Route 22, Phillipsburg

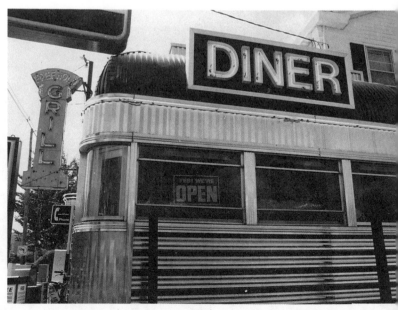

Freehold

Salem

Route 7, Belleville

Excellent Diner, Westfield

North Wildwood

SUITCASE MOTEL AND OTHER GREAT PLACES TO STAY

t's a queer little place, the green-and-white motel on Route 40 with the strange Tinkertoy-like dome on the front lawn, the bowling balls nearby, and the mystifying name in big block letters on the slanted roof: CA-NOOK.

"A lot of Canadians think we're Canuckers," Elva Cantrell says. "We're not Canadians"—she smiles—"we're United States-ians."

The motel's odd name is a contraction of her husband's name, Cantrell, and her maiden name, Cook.

"We hyphenated it to suit ourselves," Elva says.

The Ca-Nook's distinctive look—the vacant main building, once a restaurant, looks like a 1950s version of a spaceship with its upward-curving roof—is patterned after the New Mexico home the couple lived in during World War II. O'Connell Cantrell was stationed at Clovis Air Force Base; Elva Cook had been in the Signal Corps.

Wildwood

She was from Philadelphia, he was from Ashland, Kentucky, and they met one summer at a park in Pennsville.

They were married in 1944. In 1950, her uncle, who lived in Minotola, fell ill. On their way to visit him, O'Connell turned right instead of left from Route 47 onto Route 40.

"Instead of going east," Elva says, "he went west."

It was the best wrong turn O'Connell ever made. There was a For Sale sign along Route 40, and eventually the couple, along with O'Connell's brother and sister-in-law, bought the property.

"When we came here, everything was woods," Elva recalls. "The other side of the highway was woods. We came here with machetes."

O'Connell's brother and sister-in-law wanted to build a trailer park; he and Elva wanted to build a motel. The four settled on the latter.

"He wanted to get a loan," Elva says of her husband. "The bank said, 'We only give loans to farmers' sons.'"

It took O'Connell and his brother four years to build eight motel units. They finished the motel in 1957, and lived in it until the house, done in the same style, was finished in 1960.

"We built the basement, lived down there, and then moved upstairs," Elva says. "We did everything ourselves."

The restaurant didn't go over well, and O'Connell's brother and sister-in-law "wanted out, so we bought them out," Elva says. O'Connell got a job as a millwright at DuPont, where he worked twenty-eight years before retiring.

These days, O'Connell prefers to think himself as a "blue-collar physicist." A story in a local paper described him as "a backyard mechanic who thinks he knows more than Albert Einstein . . . an inventor, electrical contractor, motel operator, bicycle repairman, and millwright," not to mention "the proud father of the Spectron Grid Theory," a "relatively new, extremely complicated, almost incomprehensible explanation," the reporter noted, of the theory of gravity.

"It's just something to show off," O'Connell said of his outdoor sculpture—the big Tinkertoy dome out front, and a smaller one behind the restaurant. "I figure I want to be a physicist, which I are one."

He sometimes rambles, but Elva is always there to bring him back.

"This is junk heaven," she says as her husband pulls out photos and

The place the owners really don't want you to stay, but the people keep coming anyway. The Ca-Nook Motel, Route 40, Upper Pittsgrove

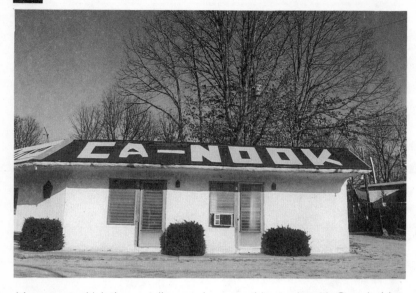

Many guests think the motel's name has something to do with Canada. Not so; it is a contraction of O'Connell's name, Cantrell, and Elva's maiden name, Cook.

O'Connell Cantrell's Tinkertoy-like dome in front of the Ca-Nook

newspaper clippings. "Anything that comes in here has stayed here."

She faithfully checks in motel guests, but sounds as if she'd rather not. After all these years, she still can't figure out why people stop at the Ca-Nook.

"People come in, I tell them there are places down the road, but they're so tired, they ask, 'Can we have a room here for the night?' I'm always amazed. We've had people from Germany, Australia, Japan, China, India. I don't know why they stop in. I wouldn't stop here myself. Just the other night, I had people from Virginia. They said every time they come up here, they stop here. I find that unbelievable."

It's not that anything's wrong with the Ca-Nook, it just looks homely and forlorn, with the handmade sign out front that says Air T.V. Heat, the boarded-up restaurant, an old message board that says simply, "Here!" At night, the only evidence anything *is* here is the dimly lit motel sign and the Coke machine shining like a beacon in front of the restaurant.

Guests generally behave themselves, but there are always a few. . . .

"People unscrew the light bulbs and take them home," Elva says. "I always wonder why that is."

The motel is located in Upper Pittsgrove; Pittsgrove is on the other side of the highway. Both are in Salem County, but mail comes from Newfield, in Gloucester County. The phone is an Elmer exchange. The Ca-Nook not only looks like something out of a time warp, it might as well be in one.

O'Connell and Elva keep just five units open, even in the summer.

"I don't want to be bothered with it anymore," Elva says.

Even though she sometimes wishes guests would go elsewhere, she and her husband are here to stay.

"This is it," she replies when asked if the couple might move some day. "We'll stay here until they take us away. We came here, we settled here." She laughs. "Even though they wouldn't give us a loan."

Route 30, Ancora

(Right) Route 33, Howell

(Far right) Benedict Motel, Route 1, Linden

Village Motel, Route 1, Rahway

Catalina Motel, Route 147, Middle Township, Cape May County

Route 130, Cinnaminson

Route 22, Lebanon

Wildwood Crest

Airport Hotel, Route 40, Atlantic City

Wildwood

Wildwood Crest

Sea Isle City

Route 22, Whitehouse

Atlantic City

Asbury Park

Seaside Heights

Route 46, west of Hackettstown

Route 47, Rio Grande

Black Horse Motel, Chews Landing

Route 607, Hopatcong

Route 57, Port Murray

Route 206, Montague

Route 46, Roxbury

Route 9, Howell

Route 30, Waterford

Wildwood Crest

MEET ME AT THE CORNER OF NIMBUS AND CUMULOUS

 hese are the roads many New Jerseyans see every day: Route 1 and Route 9; Route 3 and Route 4; Route 18 and Route 27; Route 35 and Route 36; Route 195 and Route 295; Route 280 and Route 287.

These are the roads few New Jerseyans see every day: Easy Street and Risk Avenue; Reality Drive and Daydream Lane; Grape Street and Strawberry Avenue; Bed Bug Hill Road and Bee Meadow Parkway; Sodom Lane and Pleasure Avenue; Mount Benevolence Road and Mount Misery Road; Teetertown, Tattletown, Dingletown, Flittertown, Rudetown, Scrapetown, Slacktown, and Slabtown roads.

Smile, you're on Cheerful Place.

And you don't have to be rich to live on Wealthy Avenue.

"When I explain to people what my address is, I say it's Wealthy, as in rich," says Bernie Guzman, of Wealthy Avenue, Middletown, in Monmouth County.

"You know what my address is?" James Politano says. "2 Wealthy. We picked number two not realizing it would be '2 Wealthy.' We didn't put the two together until we moved in. . . ."

"When you're ordering something by mail, it evokes a chuckle," Guzman says.

Wealthy Avenue doesn't put on the ritz. The homes here are modest; the biggest one would look small in a new suburban development. Several of the homes, in fact, are little, boxy houses that would look more appropriate on some country back road.

"In the financial sense, it's not the most wealthy, but everyone keeps their lawns up," Guzman says. "We have great neighbors. They have wealthy attitudes. They are rich in the sense of life. We feel blessed that way."

How did Wealthy get its name? You'll never guess.

"That," Barbara Eigengrauch says, "was an apple."

Her grandfather, Charles Augustus Smith, owned an orchard in the township's western end, where Route 36 is today. Look closely at the streets around Wealthy: Smith, for the family name; Lester, for Barbara's father; Baldwin, another variety of apple. And what street forms one of the intersections with Wealthy? Apple.

"The Wealthy would compare to your modern-day McIntosh, only it had more of a red blush," says Robert Eigengrauch, Barbara's husband. "It was very popular. It had a sweet-tart taste in the summer."

"It's a very old variety first selected around 1860," explains Rutgers professor Joe Goffreda of the university's Cream Ridge Fruit Research and Development Center. "The fruits are handsome in appearance, color, size, and shape," he adds, reading from a 1925 textbook. "The quality is good, the flesh being especially crisp."

The Smiths also raised peaches, and the name of one variety always raised eyebrows.

"They had pleasure telling people they had Blushing Maidens," said Middletown historian Randall Gabrielan, who also informed me that Reckless Place in Red Bank was named for Anthony Reckless, a former state senator.

Wealthy Avenue is truer to its name farther down the street, where

there are newer, more expensive homes, only there the street is known as Ravatt Road.

Politano and Guzman enjoy the reaction when they tell others where they live.

"I say, 'Wealthy,' they say, 'How do you spell it?'" Politano tells me. He laughs. "How else do you spell Wealthy?"

At the corner of Brotherhood and Fellowship, and Freedom and Justice, in Piscataway, there were once a lot of communists, socialists, and anarchists.

It was called Fellowship Farm, and it was a cooperative, drawing what one account termed "city folks eager for the green life of the country." A 1912 newspaper ad read: "A thousand dollars for a thousand hours. Get back to the land. Hear more about this at Smith and McNeil's."

Organizer George Littlefield's "Fellowship Farm Facts," a prospectus for potential members, began this way:

> Get an acre and live on it
> Get a spade and dig
> Get off the backs of the workers
> Get the shirkers off your back
> Get honest
> Get busy

"Most of them were Jewish immigrants who had left their native Russia to escape the tyranny of the czar's Cossacks, to seek freedom in America," recalled George Spayth, former publisher of the *Dunellen Chronicle,* who lived in the colony for two years. "They bore not the slightest resemblance to the popular conception of the bewhiskered anarchist with a smoking bomb in his hand."

Just across Stelton Road, another "radical" community formed: the Ferrer Colony, consisting of anarchists and "freethinkers." Among the teachers at the community's Modern School were Will Durant and Rockwell Kent.

"Here was freedom unrestrained and the colonists, who were not even carpenters, much less anarchists, proceeded to build piecemeal with their own hands a weird collection of dwellings ranging from shacks to amateur attempts at ornateness," Spayth recalled.

One of the "weird" houses remains, on School Street. It is decorated with bas-reliefs; one resident described it as "the place with arms and faces sticking out of it."

The first few seasons at Fellowship Farm were tough. Cars were almost unknown; residents would rent old Bess, the faithful farm mare, for twenty-five cents an hour to carry them to New Brunswick at what one account called the "devastating" speed of three miles an hour.

To outsiders, Fellowship Farm and the Ferrer Colony were one and the same. The two were known as the "free love colony."

"There were a lot of unfounded rumors going around," says Piscataway resident Tony Scara, whose wife, Martha, attended the Modern School.

One rumor: "That a bell rang at midnight and everyone switched wives," Scara says.

The settlers might have been a hardy bunch—the mailman made his rounds barefoot except in the coldest weather—but Fellowship Farm never became the "rural paradise" Littlefield envisioned.

"You can't do a hell of a lot of farming on those acres," recalled Karl White, who was four years old when his family moved to Fellowship Farm and who now lives in Florida. "Most of the people didn't kid themselves. A good many had jobs somewhere else."

The collective withered and died, but left its mark on Piscataway in the form of Fellowship Farm Park, the township's first municipal park; Fellowship Farm School, now a school administration building; and the North Stelton Volunteer Fire and Rescue Company, started with a donation from Fellowship Farm. The Modern School lives on, too. There is an annual reunion for former students every fall.

And the streets remain—Justice, Freedom, Fellowship, Brotherhood, Commonwealth. There was a Karl Marx Place, but it was changed to Arlington Place over the residents' protests.

"There's a lot of history in there," Scara says. "But nobody's interested in it. The people here are all yuppified. They'd all move if they found out where they live."

Off Route 30, Pomona

Wildwood

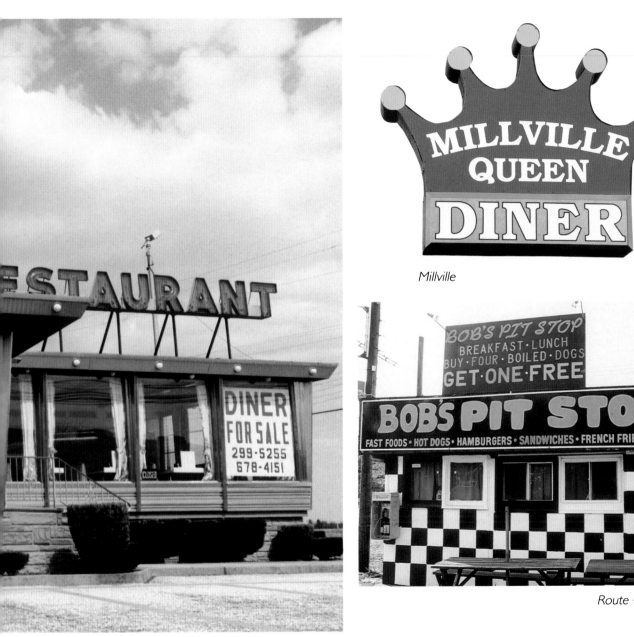

RESTAURANT

DINER
FOR SALE
299-5255
678-4151

CLOSED

Millville

MILLVILLE
QUEEN
DINER

BOB'S PIT STOP
BREAKFAST · LUNCH
BUY · FOUR · BOILED · DOGS
GET · ONE · FREE

BOBS PIT STOP
FAST FOODS · HOT DOGS · HAMBURGERS · SANDWICHES · FRENCH FRIES · COFFEE

Route 46, Garfield

Route 40, Carneys Point

Route 46, Ledgewood

Route 168, Bellmawr

North Wildwood

Wildwood

Route 40, Egg Harbor

Route 147, Middle Township,
Cape May County

Route 537, Wrightstown

Wrightstown-Cookstown Road, Cookstown

SMOKE RISE
NEXT RIGHT

REALITY DR.

Georgia
1 MILE

Hamilton Avenue, Hamilton

TODAY'S SPECIAL AT THE DOG & CAT DELI

Wildwood

When I came up with the title to this chapter, little did I know there really was a today's special at the Dog & Cat Deli.

Not just one, but four, in sample cups on the front counter of the Route 35 store in Ocean Township.

The specials:

Blackworms—"the pro's choice for live food," according to a card above the worms, which look like little noodles. "Discus, angels, and especially bottom feeders crave this aquatic worm."

Tubifex—"the steak and potatoes of live fish food, cold-water rinsed and 100 percent clean," says the card on these worms, which look like a bad case of hair drain clog.

Brine shrimp—thousands of the squiggly, wiggly things, "the fun food . . . watch your fish chase and ravish their prey!"

Glass larvae—"fresh from the cold lakes of the north, available only in the winter months."

You can get anything your pet wants at Murray Wiener's Dog & Cat Deli on Route 35, in Ocean Township, Monmouth County.

One question: Are you supposed to bring your fish in to sample these treats, or try them yourself and hope your fish takes your word for it?

"I am not considered normal, so what else but come up with godforsaken signs?" Murray Wiener says of various signs around the store, including this one in the window: "We serve cat corned beef and dog pastrami."

"People ask, 'Where's the food?'" Murray says. "We say, 'We're going to set up the tables, so bring in your dog or cat and we'll serve them in a minute.'"

He's kidding, but the Dog & Cat Deli really is a pet food take-out place. You can't get cat corned beef, but you can pick up Chick-n-Cheez Chooz, a cheese protein dog chew that you cook in the microwave; Lotsa Licks, beef jerky–like dog treats; and cookie- and chicken-wing–shaped chicken and beef treats whose "specially blended ingredients" are "oven-baked to perfection."

What else can you get at the Dog & Cat Deli? Pig ears, smoked or fried, and cows' hooves, available from bins at the front counter. Also, a "99 percent fat-free" pure beef snack food with unusual ingredients.

"You can't put in what part of the animal they're from," Murray says. He's right. I can't.

Route 22, Hillside

And don't forget Mr. Wonton, Mr. Meat, Mr. Breakfast, Mr. Shrimp, Mr. Auto Insurance, Mr. Paints, Mr. Light, Mr. Pizza, Mister Donut . . . Route 40

Also available: Sizzle Biscuits, Binzo dog treats, and Doggy News, chews in the shape of newspaper front pages.

And don't forget to pick up some pooch pacifiers, plaque attackers, and dental floss for dogs.

"Everyone knows you should floss your dog's teeth every day," Murray says.

The cat food is more mainstream, although for fat cats there is Science Diet Feline Maintenance Light.

And nothing in the dog section rivals the toilet trainer for cats that slips over the toilet bowl and includes a bag of "enticing herbs." It's called— what else—Kitty Whiz.

"Can you imagine going into the bathroom and your cat is in there screaming, 'Get out, I was in here first!'" Murray asks.

Dog & Cat Deli is a catchy name, but nothing out of the ordinary in the wacky world of New Jersey business names. Just look at the competition in the pet-store–name category alone: Pooch Palace, Debbie's Dog Dynasty, Canine Chateau, Poodle Pub, Bow Wow Heaven, Jim's Doggie Stand . . . no, wait, that's a hot-dog place in Phillipsburg.

Route 57, Franklin Township, Warren County   *Route 130, East Windsor*

Route 46, Parsippany

Dog & Cat Deli shares space with Murray's Tropiquarium, where scores of tanks hold chocolate catfish, orange skunk clowns, celestial goldfish, green terrors. Plenty of food for them, too, including Warsley Sinking Wafers, "the ultimate flake food."

Asked if he has any pets at home, Murray laughs. "When you use the word home, I get confused. I spend two-thirds of my life here. I only go home to change."

But he does have Jezebel, faithful watchdog, who can usually be found sleeping behind the front counter. About the closest she gets to vicious is a half-hearted yawn.

"Does she ever move?" I ask.

"On occasion, when there's food about," Murray says.

"Is she a good watchdog?"

"Oh, excellent. It's like, 'If you're going to burglarize the place, please do it quietly.'"

"Murray," one of his employees shouts, "did you show him the tooth-brush for dogs?"

There it is—Petrodex toothbrush and enzymatic toothpaste. In the next aisle: Crazy Balls, a psychological cat toy; Four Paws Wee-Wee Pads, and Booda Piggy Puffs, not for piggies but doggies.

"This field is absolutely unreal," Murray says. "Every day is something new."

Route 47, Vineland

Route 46, Roxbury

Newark

Route 322, Williamstown

Route 23, Butler

Carteret

Newark

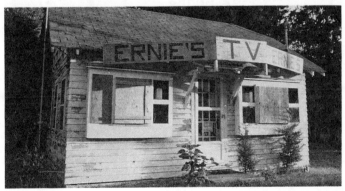

Route 9, Little Egg Harbor

Route 9, Barnegat

Jersey City

Bergenline Avenue, West New York

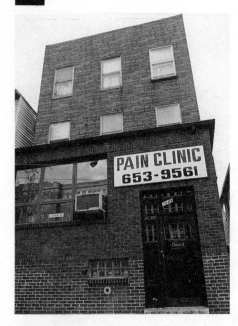

Route 1, Elizabeth

Martin Luther King Boulevard, Trenton

Bergenline Avenue, West New York

Elizabeth

Calhoun Street, Trenton

Springfield Avenue, Irvington

Route 46, White Township, Warren County

HUBCAP JACK AND OTHER ROADSIDE BUSINESSES

Route 57, Franklin Township, Warren County

 here are the pyramids at Gizeh, the Pyramid of the Sun, the Pyramid of the Moon.

And then there is the Hubcap Pyramid.

It soars twenty-five feet above Route 322 in Weymouth, a landmark to truckers and tourists (twenty-two miles to Atlantic City, forty-two miles to Philadelphia), a glittering sight when the late afternoon sun flashes off all those Ford and GM hubcaps, turning the pyramid into a roadside beacon.

Okay, so maybe it isn't the Lighthouse at Alexandria, but it is one of New Jersey's unnatural wonders.

"Even part-time, there's more damn work with these caps," Jack Lester grumbles. "Everyone rapping on my door. I can't seem to get out of it."

If he did, there would be an uproar from the customers who have depended on his highway hubcap stand the past twenty years.

It started with a few hubcaps on a pylon. Now it's a tourist attraction, admired by people on their way to or from Atlantic City. Jack Lester and his Hubcap Pyramid.

"I'm only open three days," says Jack, watching the traffic out on Route 322 from his golf cart. "The reason is that I don't want to do the footwork."

Being in his eighties has something to do with it. Ignore the grumbling; there is nothing else Jack would rather do than scoot around in his golf cart, show off the Hubcap Pyramid, prove to people he can find any cap they need. If he can't, he gives you one for free, although what anyone would do with the wrong kind of cap is not clear.

How many hubcaps does he have?

"Five thousand, ten thousand, I don't know," he says.

He once lived in Lakewood and worked as a carpenter. His last job landed him at a power plant along the Delaware River. The commute was too much; he wanted to live closer to work. A real estate agent showed him several places along Route 322, including a car repair garage with a log cabin next door that doubled as general store and local hangout.

The entire property—garage, cabin, five acres—would cost him just $16,500. The tough part was convincing his wife, Mary, who, having been raised in Bonhamton, now part of Edison, wasn't exactly a country girl.

"We had a home in a nice residential area," she says wistfully.

Jack showed her around, asked if she liked the place. She asked why. He told her he had already put a deposit down. She was not amused.

"It was real quiet when we moved in," she recalls. "I said to myself, 'Where have I moved to?'"

Historic Weymouth, twenty-two miles from Atlantic City, forty-two miles from Philadelphia, that's where. A log with that vital information is above the door of the log cabin, now Jack's hubcap headquarters. He turned the garage into his house. I stood in the kitchen talking to Mary; a pie was cooling on a rack.

"So right where we're standing . . . ?"

"Was where they repaired the cars," Mary explains.

At first, Jack sold second-hand items—shoes, rugs—from the log cabin.

"That wasn't very profitable; people would buy a trinket or two," he says.

Every once in a while, he would go to a nearby junkyard and buy parts for his pickup. The owner encouraged him to take a hubcap or two to sell back at his place.

"I'd lay them in front there. People started pulling in, 'You got a cap for this, you got a cap for that?' I thought, 'This is hotter than anything I've got.' Six months later, guy pulled in, said, 'You want some caps?' He must have had five hundred. I didn't know much about caps; I made him an offer." Jack laughs. "I was in solid. That's how I became a hubcap empire."

His empire depends on loyal subjects supplying him with hubcaps.

"I have a guy who works on the parkway, brings me caps, a guy who drives from Atlantic City to Washington, D.C., drops some off. . . ."

He started building the pyramid five years ago. It started small—a few caps on a pylon. Jack figured if he had an A-frame here and an A-frame there, he could raise them and get a . . . pyramid!

There are about one hundred caps on each side, all wired to the frame, "otherwise they'd be flopping around, blowing on the highway," Jack says.

"That pyramid is all over," Mary says. "We had people in from Hawaii last week. They took a picture of it."

This hubcap business is not for everyone. Jack's son tried it for two years. One day, he threw the keys to the place at his old man and said, "I got to pay my mortgage; I quit."

Jack's hubcap stand is open Thursdays, Fridays, and Saturdays. If he's not around when you stop by, pick out a hubcap, and leave the money.

"People stick the money under the door," Mary says. "If they don't have the money, they'll leave it the next time they stop by. It's interesting that there are still honest people today."

The log cabin is filled—"saturated," Jack says—with hubcaps. Ford caps are to the left, everything else to the right. "If you believe in credit," says a sign on the wall, "loan me five bucks."

Through a door is Jack's "warm room," an office with about a dozen clocks, including one made out of a hubcap.

Out back are several huge piles of hubcaps. If Jack doesn't have the cap you need, it probably hasn't been made.

"I don't think he's got the hubcaps I got," Jack says of EL&M, the mammoth junkyard nearby. "I've got a Rolls-Royce."

In the garage are Mary's Mustang, their son's couch, and Jack's motorcycles. At eighty-two, he still rides. Several years ago, he was stopped by a cop on the way to Tuckerton.

"He told me, 'When you took your helmet off, I thought I was going to faint,'" Jack recalls.

"He was always a daredevil, a wanderer," Mary says of her husband.

The wanderer has found a home, and the pyramid is his monument.

"It isn't quite finished," Jack says, "but there's only one person working on it."

It's a great place for a hot-dog truck: on one of New Jersey's busiest highways, across the road from the Doggie Market, and right in front of a car painting business (eat a long lunch and have your van done at the same time).

It's Cousin Freddie's Gourmet Hot Dogs, Famous Since 1957, according to the menu.

Hot dogs with anchovies, hot dogs with curry, hot dogs with peanut butter: Cousin Freddie will make the hot dog of your dreams at his truck on Route 1 in Jersey City.

"I've been alive since 1957, that's why it's famous," Fred Matise said.

How about famous along Tonnele Avenue (Route 1) in Jersey City? Matise operates Cousin Freddie's, maybe the most complete hot-dog truck in New Jersey roadside fast-food history.

"We have over one hundred combinations of hot dogs," Freddie says. "You want it with raisins and peanut butter?"

He's not kidding. Available toppings include curry, soy sauce, shallots, anchovies, green relish, Spanish olives, macadamia nuts, and spätzle, which probably should not all be ordered at once. Freddie's International Combinations hot dogs include Frahita Frank (peppers, onions, achiote, sour cream); Mexicali Mutt (chili, jalapeños, cheese, salsa), and the Puerto Rican Pup (pigo rice, bacon, saffron).

"It's an ethnic area, so you can sell ethnic things," Freddie explains.

This morning, the soup is a Japanese fish soup; tomorrow the specials would be Oriental steamed dumplings and kielbasa with sauerkraut. This is not your ordinary hot-dog truck.

"This is not a hot-dog truck," Freddie says of his vehicle, which, upon closer inspection, turns out to be a van. "We got friers, stoves, microwaves, four refrigerators. . . ."

Pots and pans, colanders, several coffee makers, fire extinguisher, and more are crammed into a tight space where Freddie and helper Will Agosta operate.

Route 322, Mullica Hill

Route 322, Cecil

"He's the resident artist," Freddie says of Will. "I do the artwork with the food, he does the artwork with the pen."

Will does a cartoon strip called "Adventures of Weiner Man"; samples hang on the wall of the Leonia deli owned by Freddie's father. Freddie worked there, then opened his own pizza place, where he apparently learned the fine art of food experimentation.

"We had all kinds of weird pizza," he recalls. "Pizza with eggs. We made a twenty-four-pound pizza. It had broccoli, cauliflower, all kinds of cheese. There was everything on that thing."

He acquired the van, formerly a catering truck, and opened Cousin Freddie's in October 1991. You want a Jersey hot dog, a Cleveland hot dog, a Southern California hot dog? Freddie will make it, even if he hasn't heard of it.

"One guy came in and wanted a Chicago hot dog," he says. "What the heck was it? Pickles, tomatoes, onions, peppers, potatoes—we do a lot of things with potatoes—mushrooms." He laughs. "The hot dog was about ten feet high when we got done."

Art Balassone, owner of DuBow's Auto Truck Painting and Freddie's landlord/partner, walked in, looking puzzled. He wanted lunch, only he didn't know what.

"Whaddya want?" Freddie asks. "BLT?"

"No."

"Sausage with onions?"

"No."

"Pizza?"

A shake of the head.

"Fajitas?"

No reply.

"How about a nice turkey and bacon?"

"What kind of cheese do you have?"

"Monterey Jack, provolone."

Artie thinks it over.

"How about pasta?" Freddie asks. "You want rigatoni with meat sauce?"

Artie starts to walk out the door. Freddie isn't about to give up.

"How about tuna?" he yells.

Artie smiles. "Tuna, melted cheese. You know how to make it."

Artie leaves. Freddie shakes his head. "I would hate to be his mother," he says.

A customer stuck his head inside the front window, looked at me and said, "He looks like a fed."

"He's investigating a murder," Will says. "Someone was clubbed to death with a hot dog."

"She wants a baked potato with a meatball," Freddie says after talking on the phone with a customer.

"What does she call that?" I ask.

"Whatever she wants."

He put the potato in the microwave, took it out and chopped up the insides, put it back in the shell ("so it looks like a lot more"), chopped up the meatball, tossed it on the potato, and poured brown gravy on top of that.

"Now we're going for presentation," he said, proceeding to peel off some red cabbage to make a bed for the potato, and for the final touch, tossing onions, carrots, and jalapeños on top.

A customer walked up and checked out the menu. "What's that, corned beef with smoked liver?" he asks.

"Exactly," Freddie says.

"That's"—the customer searches for the right word—"interesting."

Newark

*Route 206,
near Pemberton*

Route 56, Deerfield

Route 47, Dias Creek

Route 561 spur, Folsom

Route 27, Linden

Washington, Warren County

IF I HAD A (20-FOOT) HAMMER

Route 30, Egg Harbor City

 She wears a tight green skirt and gold blouse, her fingernails are painted red, her hip is slung suggestively to one side, and there is the mother of all come-hither looks on her face. She would be every guy's dream date except for one minor detail.

She is eighteen feet tall.

"We just call her the Big Broad," Ed Werbany says. "Usually when we say that, people know it. It's a landmark."

Her proper name is Miss Uniroyal, and she stands in front of Werbany's Tire Town on Route 168 in Blackwood, Camden County. She is held by two chains running from her shoulders to an overhead pole, and she stands, in black heels, on cinder blocks.

"We get some pretty strong winds down here," Werbany says. "She's held up pretty good."

She is one of a dozen or so giants looming over the Jersey landscape.

Route 22, Green Brook

ROADSIDE NEW JERSEY

There are Mr. Bill in Winslow and The Man in Jersey City, both of whom we'll meet in a while. A rugged-looking Viking stands in front of Orr's Carpeting on Route 77 in Deerfield; a leering cowboy welcomes all to Cowtown, New Jersey's only professional rodeo, outside Woodstown; a hip-looking guy in sunglasses and loud swimtrunks—call him Mr. Cool—checks out the summer crowd at WaterWorks in Seaside Heights.

But Miss Uniroyal is the most striking of them all. Built by International Fiberglass in Venice, California, she and her very big sisters were used by Uniroyal for promotions and store openings.

Hip slung suggestively to the side, the mother of all come-hither looks on her face . . . Miss Uniroyal, Route 168, Gloucester Township

Route 77, Deerfield

Route 9, Berkeley

"When you used to order tires, you would call the office and ask for Miss Uniroyal," Werbany recalls. "That's what they called the girls who filled the orders."

The only other Miss Uniroyal he knows of is in Chincoteague, Virginia.

"She's in a bikini, that one there," Werbany says. "She's at one of those miniature golf courses."

The "Big Broad" doesn't need a skimpy bathing suit to attract attention.

"I'm amazed by the number of people who stop by and take pictures of her," says Werbany sales manager John Mazzola.

"They always ask what color underwear she has on," says mechanic Frank Collison. "If a family is walking along, the son will take a look under the dress."

"She does wear underwear," Mazzola insists. "What is it, red?"

For someone so big, Miss Uniroyal takes a lot of abuse.

"We've had guys throw rocks at her, broke her, cracked her up pretty

Elizabeth

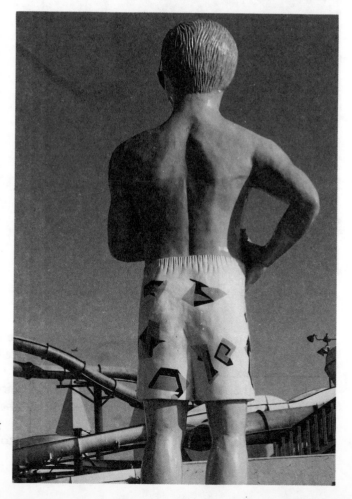

Call him Mr. Cool. He checks out the summer scene at the WaterWorks in Seaside Heights.

Route 206, Newton

Cowtown

good," Werbany says. "But we patched her up. She's going to need painting pretty soon."

He was once offered six thousand dollars for Miss Uniroyal, but declined.

"I'm not even interested in selling her," he says. "The advertising value—I can't even put a value on it."

The same can be said of Mr. Bill, the big-eared kid with the goofy grin and floppy yellow hat watching the southbound traffic on Route 561 in Winslow. Ray Giannascoli, owner of Mr. Bill's Restaurant, figures it would cost him twenty to twenty-five thousand dollars to replace the twenty-five-foot-high figure, which he bought ten years ago from the owner of a sandwich place on Route 130.

"His lease was up; they were going to demolish [the figure]," Giannascoli says. "I was looking for something as an eye-catcher here. The next week the guy calls up out of the clear blue sky and asked if I wanted it. I was only worried about one thing, getting it fixed; the company that made it went out of business. He said, 'Just take it down to a body shop.'"

The kid was trucked over in a flatbed and spent the winter in the restaurant parking lot. He was assembled in the spring.

"He's got four-inch steel pipes coming down into the ground going to six-inch pipe," Giannascoli says. "It fits in like a sleeve."

While Miss Uniroyal is chained to her post, Mr. Bill is held fast by stainless steel guide wires set in concrete. With his big jug ears and square, set shoulders, he is a formidable sight.

"My fifteen-month-old son sits out there and looks at it," Giannascoli says. "It awes him."

Mr. Bill is both landmark and highway marker—the restaurant is about halfway between Philadelphia and the shore. The restaurant was originally called Bill's Drive-In; Giannascoli renamed it Mr. Bill after the *Saturday Night Live* clay man who kept getting smacked around. Walk around behind the restaurant and you'll see a fleet of Mr. Hot Dog U.S.A. trucks. Giannascoli bought them from the original Mr. Hot Dog U.S.A., Art Maresca, who would drive his hot-dog truck, a converted 1970 Subaru, to Cowtown, auctions, and flea markets. That tiny truck is still out back, too.

The restaurant's landmark is out front, smiling at the traffic.

"Hopefully he'll be around a lot longer than I will," Giannascoli says.

Mr. Bill, on Route 561 in Winslow, is named after the Saturday Night Live character, but he's a lot more durable. The twenty-five-foot-high figure once stood in front of a sandwich shop at Route 130.

Somebody should introduce him to Miss Uniroyal. Route 30, Clementon

He looks like the lumberjack type—bearded and brawny— but the employees of Wilson's Carpet and Furniture simply call him The Man.

For landmarks, though, it would be hard to top The Man, which is what Norm Wilson and his employees call him, or Carpet Man, after what he is holding, or Paul Bunyan, which is who he looks like. The lumberjack type—big, bearded, brawny. He stands in an unlikely location—on a bend in the road where Truck 1–9 winds under the Pulaski Skyway in Jersey City.

"People call up and ask, 'Where are you located?'" says Wilson, owner of Wilson's Carpet and Furniture. "You can say Skyway, you can say 1 and 9, you can say Jersey City. But when you say the big guy holding the carpet, they know what you're talking about. You talk to truck drivers from Omaha, they use it as a landmark—the big guy when you turn under the Skyway." He laughs. "We got the giant. Carpet Giant doesn't."

Wilson bought The Man from Lafayette Sign in Jersey City, which had acquired him from the Amoco Corporation, which made such figures in two sizes, eighteen feet and twenty-five feet. Wilson put his twenty-five-foot man on the roof of his first store, and in 1990 moved him to the new location, placing a roll of carpet, made of sheet metal, in his hands.

"It was a big event, front page of the *Jersey Journal*," he recalls. "Everyone got upset when I moved it; they were [afraid they were] going to get lost."

If people get lost now, they're not looking very hard. Next to The Man is a more unlikely sight—a pair of pants. No face, no torso, just a pair of pants. Pink, no less.

"They came with the first guy, thrown in the deal," Wilson says. "I painted them pink so everyone would ask why."

Local rock groups have filmed videos around The Man; Wilson himself sat on his shoulders to film a commercial in the early 1980s. The Man is better anchored than Mr. Bill or Miss Uniroyal; Wilson had concrete poured down his pants.

"Originally we were going to put it on posts so you'd have to walk through his legs to come into the store," he says. "But you couldn't see it too well from the road."

Wilson has had "some pretty good offers," but The Man is not for sale.

"If they gave me ten thousand dollars, I couldn't put that into advertising that would do the same that it's done for me," he explains. "If you ask one hundred people in this part of Jersey, eighty would know it."

One last question: What is he going to do with that pink pair of pants?

"I don't know," Wilson replies. "I'm kind of strange that way."

Wilson Avenue, Newark

WHO'S BEEN DRINKING ON WISKEY LANE?

 iskey Lane instead of Whiskey Lane. Woodwman Avenue instead of Woodman Avenue. "Condos 4 Sail." "We Gladely Accept Food Stamps." "Buisiness for Sale."

Can't anybody spell around here?

There's a street in Hammonton, off Route 54, named Woodman. For several months, though, one side of the street sign read "Woodman," the other "Woodwman." The incredible thing was that nobody noticed the error, or reported it, until yours truly, a charter member of the New Jersey Properly Spelled Streets Commission, brought it to light.

"It's supposed to be spelled 'Woodman,' but it's not," I told a city employee.

"I didn't know that!" she said cheerily. "You're a very observant person."

CONDO'S 4 SAIL
APT'S.
A- 4
B- 3
C- 2
C- 4
E- 3
945-5300
OPEN HOUSE
INSPECTION

North Bergen

"You're kidding," said Public Works Director Anthony Scaffidi.

"No," I said.

"It's wrong. I've got to take it down."

"Didn't you know it was there?"

"I didn't notice and I drive by there every day," Scaffidi said. "I'm glad you brought it to my attention. No one has said anything about it."

I told him exactly where the sign was, and he promised to check it out. The next day, I called Scaffidi to find out what had happened.

"I went to the end of the street; there was nothing wrong," he said.

"It's not at the end of the street, it's at the beginning, at the corner," I said.

"I thought you were pulling my leg," he said.

"I wasn't pulling your leg."

"People have done it."

A week later, I called again. Scaffidi had discovered that someone in his crew had made the mistake.

"He was embarrassed. He thought he had a *m*. He had a damn *w*."

That still didn't explain why there was both a *w* and an *m,* but I didn't press it.

"I'm glad you noticed it and not somebody like the mayor," Scaffidi said.

You won't find this sign in Hammonton anymore. The city public works director had it changed after I brought it to his attention.

Which brings us to Wiskey Lane. Not Whiskey Lane, Wiskey Lane, off Route 12 in Hunterdon County. Probably named for the cider or apple brandy—called apple whiskey in colonial times—once made around here.

The misspelled street sign has been up some fifteen years, and may be up fifteen more. In fact, the sign has been replaced three times, and it has been misspelled every time. Who's responsible for the error? No one wants to admit it.

"We called when they first put the sign up." said Howard Greenwald, owner of Bradford Press, a printer located on Whiskey Lane. "They said, 'It's not misspelled at all. If it is, it's the sign company's fault.' It's been continually misspelled. I think pride has gotten in the way of somebody's wisdom."

I called up the Franklin Township clerk's office. Someone there told me to check neighboring Kingwood because the street was located there.

"The part I'm talking about is in Franklin," I said.

Route 12, Franklin Township, Hunterdon County. The sign has been up some fifteen years, and may be up fifteen more.

"A teeny part is in Franklin," she said. She told me to try the township public works department.

"It's probably just misspelled," was the reply from a department employee, who then said: "I don't know if that's the right spelling or not."

"It's not."

He told me to call public works supervisor Alan Dilly.

"To tell you the truth, I don't know," Dilly said. "I've only been here six years. I could make up a good story. . . ."

A month later, I called Dilly again.

"I talked to one of our commissioners; he's been here a long time," he said. "He doesn't know. You're the first person who ever saw it or mentioned it. I know Whiskey is spelled with an *h*. That's spelled with an *i*."

I called up the street sign company that made the sign.

"Municipalities fax us their lists—they precipitated it," said an angry company official. "We don't spell Whiskey Wiskey."

"I'm a printer; this is embarrassing," said Greenwald, who said he was tempted to make up a carat in his shop, place it between the *W* and *i* on the sign, and insert the missing *h*.

"If I made a mistake, I would have to stand for it," he said. "Nobody is standing for this."

I called him several weeks later to tell him of Dilly's apparent reluctance to change the sign.

"No one takes a risk," Greenwald said, laughing. "We're so laid back here."

Route 168, Chews Landing

A few years ago, this road sign appeared on Route 130 in South Brunswick: South River Cranbepry Road.

It's one thing to spell Cranbury (the proper name for the road) Cranberry, but Cranbepry?

Tracking down the person responsible for the mistake was not easy.

"We don't make the signs; we get them from somewhere else," said an employee of the construction company fixing the road. "They probably got them wrong and sent them to us."

An hour later, I talked to another worker at the same company.

"We give the order, another company makes the sign up," he explained.

Route 23

"Sometimes there's a mistake, someone hears it wrong over the phone, translates it wrong. It happens. But I don't know how they got the *p* and *r*."

He joked that the sign served at least one useful purpose—"It keeps people awake. Helps them make sure they're on the right road."

A half hour later, the company owner called. I told him how Cranbury was spelled. He was not amused. I finally tracked down the sign company and, to my amazement, found someone who admitted the mistake.

"I did it," said a guy who said his name was Hank.

"How did you do it?"

"I live in Toms River. Down there, we have a lot of cranberry bogs. That's the way I spelled it."

"But it's still not close. It's spelled 'Cranbepry.'"

"Nah, nah," he said, not believing me. He finally did.

"Berry you could get away with," he added. "How was it spelled? Betry?"

"No. Bepry."

"Now I know why they were creating such a big fuss."

Route 49, Quinton

Springfield Avenue, Irvington

Main Street, Bound Brook

Hamilton Street, Somerset

Route 94, Fredon

Off Route 18, East Brunswick

Route 31, Clinton

Route 40, Egg Harbor

Belmar

Route 555, Cross Keys

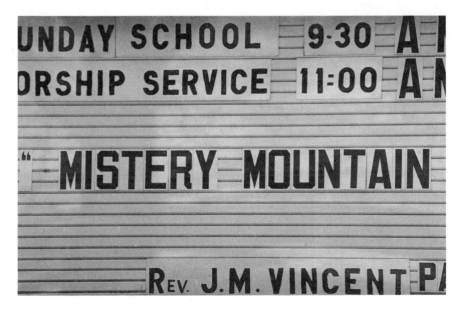

South Bound Brook

Route 9, Ocean View

HELP!
(ROADSIDE MESSAGES II)

What freezes second?

 ot long ago, along Route 46 in Warren County, there was this curious message on a board tied to a tree:

HELP.

No one in the house needed any help. The tree did, though.

"There's a lot of people sympathetic to this," Helen Ertl says. "It's not just this crazy lady."

All the "crazy lady" wanted to do was save the tree with the HELP sign on it, plus ten others in Vienna, three miles from Hackettstown.

The trees, all maples, form a natural archway over the center of town. They stand in the way, though, of progress, namely the widening of the two-lane bridge over the Pequest River.

No one here contested the fact the bridge needed repair, but many believed the project didn't have to come at the expense of the trees.

After hearing of the state Department of Transportation's plans, Helen

The sign in front of the Ertl house in Vienna shows residents' efforts to save the maple trees.

formed a citizens' group. Members drafted letters, circulated a petition, attended meetings.

"Every time we talk to DOT, they say, 'You can only talk about your trees,'" Helen says. "One [DOT official] said, 'Well, they're old trees.'"

For the Ertls, it was not just a matter of saving some old trees, but preserving New Jersey's rural beauty and identity. In 1880, Vienna was a village "with a large local trade, a foundry, a chair factory, a hotel," according to one account. The foundry, which made corn plows, was the Vienna Foundry, after which the town is named.

Fred Ertl, sitting in his sunny kitchen, hands me a sepia-tinted postcard from 1911 titled, "Bridge Over the Pequest—Vienna." The big tree in the postcard, Fred says, is still there.

"They say, 'Oh, Helen Ertl and her trees,'" his wife says. "It's not my tree. . . . It's like Budd Lake. They took the trees down there. That's what's going to happen here. They did it in Budd Lake, they did it in so many places. I just said, 'Stop.'"

The petition, she says, was signed by "quite a few hundred" people, both residents and out-of-towners. "This plan will destroy the beauty of another little hamlet in New Jersey," it read. "What we need is a bridge repaired or built that is the same in conspicuous size. There is no need for a larger bridge. . . . Massive, beautiful, irreplaceable trees will be cut down. Make the right decision to stop DOT from making an error in judgment that will be another scar on our Garden State."

A temporary roadway will be built on either side of the bridge while it is being replaced. The roadway will be tapered back onto Route 46; the taper as originally planned ran right through the trees, which meant they had to be cut down.

"I can understand the value of these trees to the town," says senior DOT engineer Scott Thorn. "It makes their community look nice. But it is something that has to be done."

The trees, he points out, stand on state right-of-way.

Members of the citizens' group each took several letters of the alphabet from the phone book and started calling people, trying to drum up support. Hackettstown Brownie Troop 109 "adopted" the 120-year-old trees; the girls put their names on plaques, which they then tied to the trees.

There was some irony in the fact that Vienna is part of Independence Township—"scenic" Independence, according to welcome signs leading into the twenty-square-mile municipality.

"It hurts," says Fred Ertl, proudly showing the "1882" carved above his barn door. "Here they go again. They just smash and crash through things. They don't realize what they're doing to New Jersey."

"They think the people they're associating with are country bumpkins," says Helen, who, like her husband, grew up in Jersey City.

But all the phone calls and petition signatures paid off—somewhat. The DOT later announced it would downsize the project, shrinking the taper of the road. Five of the maples would be saved.

"They are still in what we call the clear zone," Thorn says. "Yes, they are still an obstacle. Yes, they still can be hit [by vehicles]. If we have to do improvements to the road [in the future], they will have to come down.

"We don't sit here and try to do these things," he adds. "We have to keep the state moving."

"What they're doing is destroying the beauty of New Jersey," Helen says. "The small towns are so important. Don't they care?"

Fred looks at his wife, at the letters and clippings on the dining room table. "You gave them a good fight," he says.

Route 23, Colesville

Phillipsburg

South Broad Street, Trenton

Perry Street, Trenton

Route 561, Winslow

Route 30, Hammonton

Route 30, Mullica

East State Street, Trenton

Route 35, Wall

Route 46, Ledgewood

Route 9, Bayville

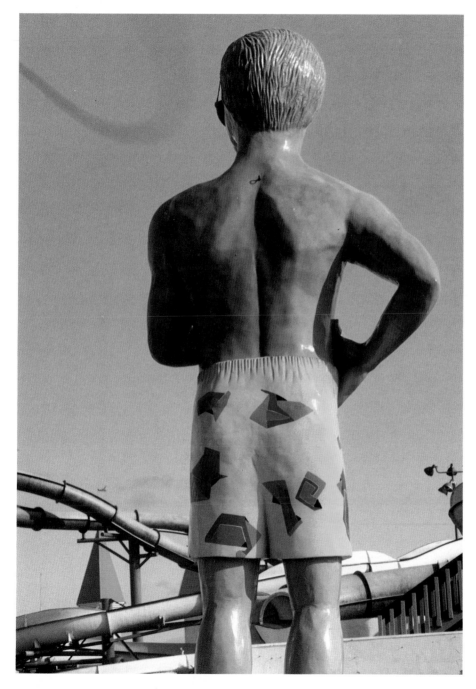

Nice shorts. WaterWorks, Seaside Heights

Asbury Park

Route 27, Somerset

Route 46, Ledgewood circle

Route 130, Bordentown

Wildwood

Route 1, Jersey City

Clinton Avenue, Trenton

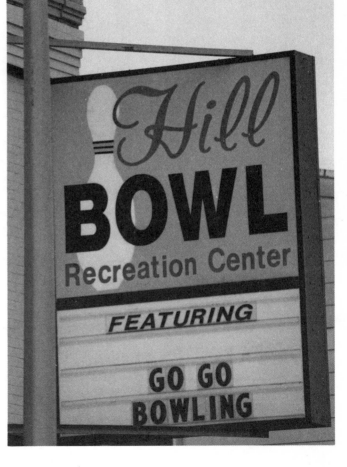

Carteret

Off Route 551, Carneys Point

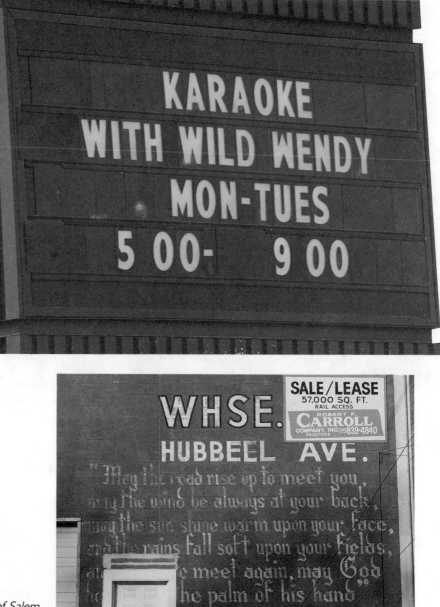

Route 517, Tewksbury

An Erdner warehouse in the town of Salem

PARKING FOR **QUIET MAN** ONLY

AND OPTOMETRIST

Route 46, Dover

"Stopping at 3rd base. adds nothing to the score. Go all the way"

ABE FROST 8·1·77

One of several homespun messages written on the side of the Erdner warehouses on Route 45 in Woodstown. Earl Erdner took the sayings from friends, from things he had seen or heard, "from all over the place," his granddaughter once recalled.

Route 41, Turnersville

Sign in the Pine Barrens

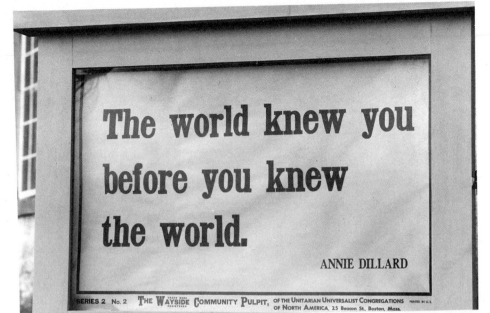

The world knew you before you knew the world.

ANNIE DILLARD

SERIES 2 No. 2 THE WAYSIDE COMMUNITY PULPIT, OF THE UNITARIAN UNIVERSALIST CONGREGATIONS OF NORTH AMERICA, 25 Beacon St, Boston, Mass.

Route 579, Kingwood

WE FIX WATER

Route 33, Manalapan

Hackettstown

This was a billboard on Route 22, Hillside, advertising a TV show. Someone switched the panels and garbled the message.

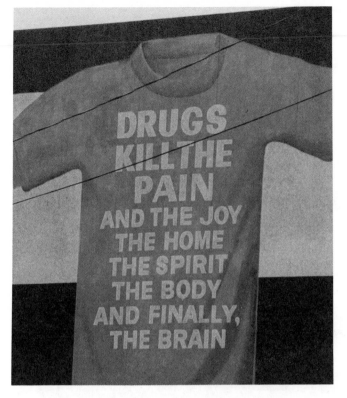

A billboard on Route 322 put up by the Baha'i faith

Route 30, Camden

Route 54, Hammonton

Route 538, South Harrison, Salem County

Belmar

Main Street, Shiloh

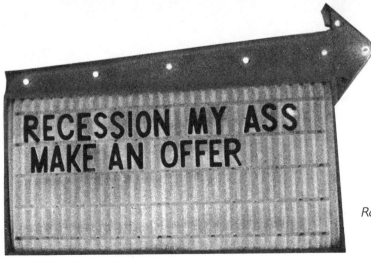

Route 73, Pennsauken

Route 31, Raritan Township

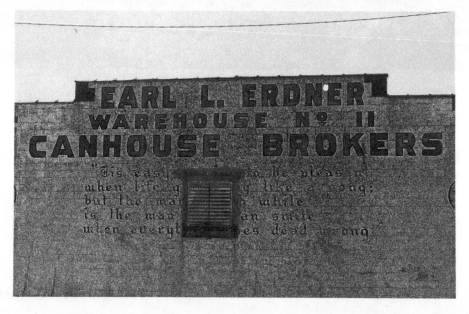

Route 45, Woodstown

Route 46, Morris County

Route 30, Ancora

Long Beach Island

2,093 BOTTLES OF MILK ON THE LAWN, 2,093 BOTTLES OF MILK...

Route 35, Neptune

 t's one thing to have a bunch of milk jugs on your front lawn. It's another to know you have exactly 2,093 of them.

"I have to keep track of them," Josephine Stapleton says. "People always ask me that question."

They've been asking the Mays Landing resident that question for thirty-one years, which is how long Josephine has been decorating the front lawn of her Route 40 home with the different-colored milk jugs.

Anyone who drives down this stretch of Route 40 and does not notice 2,093 milk jugs on somebody's front lawn is concentrating entirely too much on the road. On the other hand, many people have noticed the jugs over the years and still haven't quite figured out what they are.

"I had Saudi Arabian people stop here once," Josephine says. "You know what they wanted? Apple cider. They saw the color and thought it was apple cider. I said, 'If you drink what's in the bottle, you'll drop over dead.'"

Josephine Stapleton and her milk jugs

The jugs are filled with what looks like different fruit juices but is actually water dyed by Josephine. She uses McCormick Food Color for four basic colors—red, green, blue, and yellow—Tintex Fabric Dye for orange, and combinations of the five for other colors.

Fine, but why different colors? Well, you can't make an American flag without red, white, and blue. The milk-jug flag is the main attraction on her front lawn, the permanent exhibit in her roadside gallery. And of course Josephine knows how many jugs it took to make that flag.

"There should be 806," she says. "You take 31 [rows across] by 26 [rows down]."

What would possess someone to cover her front lawn with milk jugs as opposed to, say, flowers?

"I started this because my sons wouldn't stay off the grass with their bikes and mini-bikes and dune buggies," Josephine explains. "They used to run around the house. They didn't have to mow the grass, I did. I thought of cement blocks to keep them out but cement blocks cost money. We drink so much milk that one day I got this brainy idea."

Milk jugs. Plentiful, cheap, and, arranged in the right way, works of art.

She saved "about 372" jugs on her own, then relatives started dropping them off.

"I have a brother-in-law who brings me bottles every seven or eight days," she says. "He drinks the low fat."

Soon, passers-by were dropping jugs off, or mailing them when they returned home.

"People from Maryland, Pennsylvania, Virginia, just people coming by," she says. "One fellow said, 'Do you want a bottle from Wisconsin?' I said, 'Sure.' He said, 'It's not a milk bottle.' I said, 'I don't care.'"

She had Wawa jugs, Cloverland Dairy jugs, Great Bear Water jugs, all kinds of jugs. By May 1992, she had accumulated enough jugs and containers to make a flag for Flag Day. Just before the big event, a local kid intentionally drove his truck up on the lawn, cutting a swath through the jugs. Josephine says the kid had a "grudge" against her son.

"I lost 600 out of 800 bottles," she recalls, standing on her front lawn. "They just wiped it out. I cried for two weeks. I couldn't even come out here. It was like looking at a cemetery plot. That was how hard it hit me."

She hasn't had any more trouble from kids; all she has to do now is battle the elements.

"A hailstorm came by and busted my jugs," she says a few weeks after I first talked to her. "Half the flag was destroyed. I went through thirty trash bags. Do you know what day it was? April Fool's Day. Would you believe it?"

She has gone to other milk-jug creations, including a pumpkin for Halloween, a turkey for Thanksgiving, Santa Claus for Christmas. She embellishes the scene with beautiful needlepoint—a leprechaun for St. Patrick's Day, a rabbit for Easter.

"It's like an artist," she says. "I start the design, I have to walk away and look at it. If it don't look right, I can tell right away."

It's a full-time job, being a milk-jug artist.

"As soon as the weather breaks, I'm out here twelve hours a day," she says. "I bring the phone out, the radio. Anybody wants me, they know I'm out here."

Route 561 spur, Folsom

Her dream is to one day make a milk-jug United States on her front lawn, using a jug from each state. She has a long way to go, having jugs from just a half dozen states. She has more immediate concerns, anyway. A retired Mays Landing school bus driver, she worked as a shuttle bus driver for Atlantis Casino until it folded. She has applied for dozens of jobs—at local stores, bakeries—but no one, she says, has called her.

"I need a job, I need a job bad," she says. "Nobody wants me."

Next to the flag on the front lawn is another of her creations, fashioned not of milk jugs but bricks, shiny yellow tablecloth, and Christmas tree garland. It is Josephine's pot of gold.

Is.
Isn't
Is.
Isn't.

The question has been raging back and forth across New York Bay for years: Is the Statue of Liberty in New York or New Jersey?

"Obviously New York," say city officials, arguing that people have always associated the statue and nearby Ellis Island with the Big Apple.

"Obviously New Jersey," counter officials from the Garden State, pointing to the map—any map!—that clearly shows the statue much closer to New Jersey.

Well, there is an indisputable answer to the age-old question. Just get on the New Jersey Turnpike, get off at Exit 3, take Route 42 south and then Route 55 south, and get off in . . . Vineland?

"There's not a day you're out there when someone doesn't stop along the road," says Raymond Sotnychuk.

What is everyone looking at? The Statue of Liberty. About two stories high, sitting in the Sotnychuks' backyard. No, they didn't build it, they tell visitors. It was there when they bought the house.

Her creater was George Arbuckel. He was "just a plumber," or at least that was the way he described himself to reporters. But his Statue of Liberty—for a time, it was electrified—and the ornamental lions, the nymph-bedecked fountains, and the messages written in the walkways (Chief Rolling Water Black Feet Trail, Indian Park) attracted crowds.

Route 40, Pittsgrove

The Statue of Liberty really is in New Jersey. She can be seen in the back yard of a home on Main Road (Route 555) in Vineland.

"When newspapermen came down from New York and Philly, he said he didn't know what they were making a fuss about," Sotnychuk says. "He told them he wasn't a builder, just a plumber. When he built the fountain, he draped it in burlap, so no one knew what was going on."

Arbuckel inscribed it the Fountain of Youth, but with its statuary, it looks more like the Fountain of Lions.

"He was quite a character," says Sotnychuk, standing in front of Miss

Liberty. "He used to raise canaries, amaryllis bulbs. Kept horses . . ."

"Heating expert, political pundit, self-styled amateur psychologist, and overall seeker of the unusual," was the way a *Vineland Times Journal* reporter described Arbuckel.

"The 'unusual' included spiritualism and astrology," wrote Holly Metz and Robert Foster, authors of *Two Arks, a Palace, Some Robots, and Mr. Freedom's Fabulous Fifty Acres*, the wonderful catalog that accompanied their show on grass-roots art at the Jersey City Museum several years ago. "Arbuckel also debated psychology with scholars from the Vineland Training School, later renamed the American Institute for Mental Studies," according to Metz and Foster. "He attempted astrological matchmaking for his children, but they rejected his conclusions."

A neighbor told Sotnychuk that Arbuckel conducted séances inside the house. After a day's work, Arbuckel would invite the father of his right-hand man, Leon Hutchinson, into the séance room "to talk to the dead."

The Arbuckel house was not the only peculiar home in Vineland. The "strangest house in the world" was here, too. It was George Daynor's Palace of Depression, a "multicolored 18-spire castle made from clay, concrete, and automobile parts," according to Metz and Foster, who included it in their catalog.

The idea came to Daynor in a dream, in which an angel told him to build "a home, a haven of peace, away from bread lines and all such depressing phenomena," according to one account. The Palace of Depression was visited by as many as 250,000 people in the 1930s and '40s.

But Arbuckel's home, unlike Daynor's, remains. Arbuckel's granddaughter Debbie Minton told Metz that Arbuckel was not a social outcast, that the family "belonged to societies and organizations" in town. Arbuckel died in 1948 at the age of seventy-two. The Sotnychuks bought the property two years later, and have kept the lions and nymphs in good condition. Raymond's sister, Linda, was married under the Statue of Liberty, the one that is indisputably in New Jersey.

Raymond drives down from the city on weekends to visit his mother and say hello to a menagerie that probably would have made Arbuckel happy—chickens, geese, turkeys, and German shepherds named Rascal, Cleo, Pharaoh, and Tut. Watching over all is Miss Liberty, serene, almost Buddha-like.

Route 322, Penny Pot

Route 40, Landisville

Route 322, Hamilton, Atlantic County

Pequest Road, Mansfield

Route 559, English Creek

Route 30, Pomona

Route 33, Howell

Sea Breeze, about as far from "New Jersey" as you can get.

Route 9, Lakewood

WORLD'S BEST BIGGEST FINEST MOST FAMOUS

Route 47, Middle Township

 here can the world's best sub, the world's best spaghetti, the world's nicest sandwich, the world's biggest ice cream cone, and world-famous crabs, cheesesteaks, chili dogs, peanut brittle, malted waffles, and milkshakes be found?

New Jersey. And forty-nine other states.

Seems like every town in America boasts at least one restaurant with a "world's best" this or "world famous" that on the menu. I hate to break the bad news, but most of these places are legends in their own minds.

"Is it the world's best sub or what?" I ask an employee at a sub shop near Great Adventure claiming the world's best sub.

"Well . . ." he says, laughing.

What about the "world's best spaghetti," served at Maplewood IV Restaurant in Waterford?

"I think it's good, but I'm no expert," a waitress says. "I'm Irish."

World's best this, world-famous that: Most of the places that make such claims are legends in their own minds. But Display World in Monroe, Middlesex County, really does have the world's largest collection of stone.

And the "world-famous malted waffle" at Joe's Chadwick Diner at the shore?

"Let the waffle," an employee says, "speak for itself."

"There are a million places in New Jersey that say world's best or world's largest," says Lou Rothman. "We may be the only ones who really are the world's largest."

Rothman is owner of JR Tobacco, "the world's largest cigar store," which is written in big letters across the Fairfield store. Actually, the eight stores in the nationwide chain comprise the world's largest cigar store. The chain sells 40 percent of the handmade cigars in America.

So is there a true "world's largest" in New Jersey? Well, along Spotswood-Englishtown Road in Monroe, there is Display World, "the world's largest stone museum."

Really.

"We have the largest collection of stone in the world; I know for a fact," the Greek says. "People come from all over the world."

The Greek is the Greek; no one around Display World calls him anything else. He is so much the Greek that at a dinner in his honor someone actually introduced him by his real name and he didn't stand up until a friend poked him and said, 'Get up, stupid, that's you.'"

The stones at Display World aren't diamonds and rubies, although some are rare. There are no armed guards patrolling the showroom and you don't need an appointment. In fact, this is largely a drive-through museum.

The Greek is a landscaper. The world's largest stone museum, open seven days a week, admission free, is a museum of landscape stone: Tennessee variegated strip rubble and Multi-Color No. 57, Jerusalem stone and Mexican beach pebbles (use them in your fish tank or on your driveway), Delaware River gravel, mason sand, and a thousand other kinds.

Colorful sign marking the way to Greek's Playland at Display World

Route 130, Westville

"Some people have crystal balls and donkeys and Madonnas on their front lawns," the Greek says. "I don't do that."

What he does is stone: stone from seventy-plus suppliers, all neatly arranged and numbered in the Greek's unique showroom—a half-mile-long sheltered path ringing an artificial lake, complete with waterfalls and bridges.

The lake is the centerpiece of what to Greek is more important than the world's largest stone museum. It is Greek's Playland, jammed in summer by groups of handicapped adults and children from state homes.

"We cater to the retarded adults because they don't have anybody," the Greek explains. "Nobody invites them anywhere because everyone's afraid of them."

More than seven hundred outings have been held here since 1976, when the Greek opened his Playland. The outings don't cost the state anything; the Greek provides food and beverages free.

"People don't believe it—they think it's a gimmick," he says. "We don't accept gifts. Everything is free. Why do people think it's a gimmick?"

Why does he do it? The Greek is an orphan; he was raised by a woman

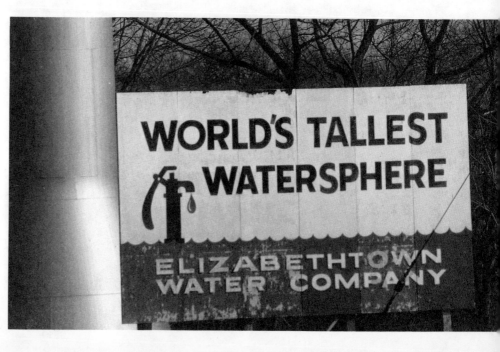

Off the Garden State Parkway, Union

Route 559, Gravelly Run

who took in some sixty kids over the years. "She always had ten or twelve of us at a time," he recalls. "I always said if I ever had money, I'd give half of it to charity."

And landscaping has given him plenty of money. There was a time he would "take fifty grand and go on vacation." He talks about having dinner with Prince Rainier in Monaco, of heli-skiing with the shah of Iran. It's not easy believing that someone who dresses in flannel shirts and laborer's pants skied with the shah, but the Greek apparently once lived life in the fast lane.

"Now I just go to conventions," he says. "There's nothing materialistic I need. I don't need cars. I don't own jewelry. Wait, I have one piece of jewelry. I don't have a watch. I have two suits . . . I really don't have anything. People don't believe me. I either lost it or gave it away."

His clients have included Jon Bon Jovi and rock music promoter Don Kirshner, and one day New Jersey's biggest rock star called.

"Bruce Springsteen wanted me to come out on a Sunday, but I told him I had to pick up my kids," Greek recalls. "I asked them, 'You ever hear of a guy named Bruce Spring-something?' They couldn't believe it. They said, 'You told Bruce Springsteen you were busy?'"

The Greek hopes to turn Playland into an amusement park, with boat rides, miniature golf, batting cages, and other attractions. The park mascot is already in place: a thirty-foot-high clown with telephone poles for legs, an oil tank for a torso, and an air conditioner for a hat. A clown made out of junk.

"This was all made with waste product," Greek says, driving around the property. "See those tires?" He points to brightly painted tires welded together for kids to scamper around. "They're twenty years old."

Those huge blocks over there? Replaced sections of the George Washington Bridge. "They didn't know what to do with them," he says. "I bought them for $250 apiece." He uses them as holding bins for stone.

And the 1,600 guardrails he bought from the Garden State Parkway? Greek uses them to make bins and structural supports.

The thirty-foot-high clown towers over the second of two lakes on the property. There is a constant problem with geese fouling the water, so Greek had artificial swans made and installed in the water, along with speakers through which he plays swan calls. He even paints and replaces the swans so the geese don't one day realize that the same old swans have been out there year after year.

The world's largest stone museum, which also boasts the "largest collection of pool tiles and pool copings in the world," according to the Greek, includes a rock museum.

Not the world's largest, by any means, but assembled in world-record time—three weeks. There are rows and rows of colorful rock: lapis lazuli, adventurine, black onyx, Botswana agate. One dollar each, the rocks are a big hit with kids. The front counter and shelves are stocked with jewelry, fossils, and more rock: amethyst clusters from Brazil, orange calcite from Mexico, meteorites from Czechoslovakia.

The star attraction is a 350-million-year-old Devonian fossil plate, as big as a small table, from the Atlas Mountains in Morocco.

The "curator" of the not-yet-world-famous rock museum is Jerry Kleiner, a part-time teacher who describes himself as "sort of the public relations man for the Greek."

Kleiner sees the museum expanding, although where—it adjoins the office—is not immediately clear. "Underground," he says, and he may not be kidding.

A meteorite from Arizona will be welded onto a post and displayed out

HOME OF THE WORLD'S NICEST SANDWICH SINCE 1979

South Seaside Park

front. There are several huge rocks on poles along the road; many people mistake them for fake rocks.

Anyone in need of a quick rock education, this is the place. An outdoor display explains The Three Types of Rock on This Planet; a chart inside groups forty kinds of rock by their New Age properties, as compiled by Agatha "Aggie" Keith.

Fluorite, one learns, "improves memory and concentration, helps mental clarity," which is why it is known as the "student stone." Snowflake obsidian, the "unhexing" stone, "helps remove whammies and bring good luck."

The Greek loves all this stuff; here is a man who never fails to be fascinated by the wonderful world of rock and stone.

"They have one brick that's the prettiest brick you've ever seen," he says. "You know what it's made of? Cow shit! They put it in a kiln, it explodes or something, and it makes these weird, beautiful colors."

There are more than one thousand kinds of landscape stone here, but Greek hopes to have ten thousand, if not more, eventually on display.

"Right now, we're the largest in the world, and we're going to make sure it stays that way," he says.

Route 130, Haddon

Route 33, Freehold

Route 503, Hackensack

Route 35, Chadwick Beach

Route 40, Mays Landing

Route 37, Pelican Island

Route 37, Toms River

Roadside shrine to fallen state trooper, Route 78 West, near the Summit exit

Route 49, Salem County

Route 30, Hammonton

Warinanco Park, Roselle

Trenton

West Milford

The author took this picture but forgot to write down the location. Do you know where I am?

Main Avenue, Paterson

Route 36, Hazlet

Route 54, Buena Vista

Need a wrench? This Bill Clark sculpture has one, plus gears, fan blades, wheels, and other bits and pieces in its junkyard-parts body. EL&M Automotive, Route 640, Hammonton

Brunswick Avenue, Trenton

Route 643, Weekstown

Route 47, Dias Creek

Route 30, Haddon Heights

Route 559, Gravelly Run

Gibbstown, Gloucester County

Trinity United Methodist Church, Route 47, South Dennis

THE DETOURS
OF SIN

Surf City

he claim checks Gus Pappas dispenses from his parking lot at
the corner of Ohio and Atlantic avenues in Atlantic City con-
tain the usual disclaimers about management not being responsible for loss, theft, etc. That's the small print. The large
print is devoted to Scripture passages—one on the front, one on the back.

This is, after all, Praise the Lord Parking.

"People ask, 'What kind of parking lot do you have with God?'" Gus
says. "Sinners get mad at the sign, devils get mad. I didn't put it up. God
helped me put it up. I wouldn't have had the guts to put it up without Him."

The sign causes double-takes even in Atlantic City, where you'll see
anything if you stay long enough. Gus's regular customers—most work in
the casinos or in a school around the corner—don't seem to mind. The
sign doesn't discourage business; the lot is jammed this particular winter
afternoon.

"The sign says to the people, 'Jesus is Lord,'" Gus explains.

He stands in his booth on this bitter cold day; the only heat comes from a portable unit that barely keeps one's feet warm. Everything Gus needs is inside—refrigerator, pots and pans, hot plate, cooking oil, packages of ketchup from McDonald's, an old couch covered with towels—and dozens of small Bibles he hands out to those interested. A sign on the window says Jesus is the Reason for the Season. Gus's lunch is on a counter—banana, two slices of pizza, chocolate milk.

Gus is wrapped in a parka and wears large owlish glasses; a day's growth of beard is on his face. If you saw him on the street, you might mistake him for a homeless man, or at least someone you wouldn't ordinarily strike up a conversation with.

But ten years ago, Gus Pappas owned a diner—right on this spot. Born in Greece, he came to this country when he was eighteen. He married, moved to Farmingdale, ran a diner on Route 33. One day in Atlantic City, he saw that the diner here, the Apollo, was for sale. It had gone bankrupt.

Gus bought it at a "very reasonable" price and ran it from 1974 to 1979, when it burned down.

"I was going to put up another, but there was a need for parking lots," he explains. "Casinos were putting up the high-rises."

In 1984, a customer gave him a Bible, and it changed his life.

"I was a sinner, I was living like everyone else . . . I was a gambler," he says, watching cars pull in and out of the lot. "I used to go to church, go for a good time, see the girls. I used to go to the casinos. Those two don't go together.

"Someone gave me a Bible, and I believed. I read the Bible, I realized how much I needed the Savior. I asked Jesus to come into my heart. What I got is eternal life. Everything else"—snaps his fingers—"is nothing."

He had his Praise the Lord Parking sign made up, and ordered Bibles—"they're very cheap"—from the American Bible Society. Bibles not just in English, but Spanish, Greek, and other languages.

"The devil—this is his kingdom here yet," Gus says. "That's why you see killings, fighting, and jealousy. But my God is bigger than the devil. Amen. When the devil comes to give it to me, I can smile because my God is bigger."

He goes out to rearrange a half dozen cars so that the teachers from

Gus Pappas once operated a diner at the spot. Now he runs Praise the Lord Parking, handing out free Bibles to anyone who shows an interest. Atlantic City

the school around the corner can get out of the jammed lot. Two men, foreign tourists, walk up to the booth.

"What nationality are you?" Gus asks.

"Belgium," one replies.

"Belgium," Gus says. "What are you doing here?"

"To lose money. What else is anyone here for?"

"Time is very short," Gus says after they leave. "The Lord is coming back very, very soon. We have to get ready."

"What do you mean?"

"He is coming back. We have to realize we are sinners. We have to repent for our sins. He's coming back. We are in the last days. I believe that with all my heart. Get ready."

He goes out to rearrange more cars. A short time later, I prepare to leave.

"Will you get a good story?" Gus asks.

"I think so. Thanks."

"Praise God." He points his finger heavenward. "I will see you up there."

Route 519, Frankford, Sussex County

Twenty-five miles and another world from Praise the Lord Parking, at a bend in the road deep in the Pine Barrens, the faithful have gathered for the Sunday service at Jenkins Chapel. There is Dave Cavileer, the lay minister; Bob Hagaman, the regular pastor; Marge Fox, the organist; a man who lives in a nearby trailer park; and myself. There are several lines on a board on the wall: Number on Roll, Attendance Today, Attendance Last Sunday. The number next to the last line: 3.

"It's been up and down," Hagaman says of the attendance at his little mission in the pines. "We went up to twelve and fifteen for a few years, then it went down. We're between four and six now."

The chapel, with twenty-eight chairs, may be the smallest church in New Jersey; its setting is certainly one of the most beautiful. It sits above Route 563 in a clearing; the sun streams through the trees that encircle the chapel. A board with the time of Sunday service—10:45 A.M.—hangs from a hand-hewn post out front. The "driveway" is a sandy path dotted with pine cones; you park on the shoulder of the road and walk up.

"There are times when I'm the only one here," Hagaman says. "But we've always kept the door open."

Etched in the foundation stone, to the left of the door, is the date August 12, 1900. The Episcopal Diocese of New Jersey originally ran the chapel as one of four Missions in the Pines.

But after the last pastor retired, the diocese closed up Jenkins Chapel. Carl Farrell, pastor of the Methodist Church's so-called Lower Bank circuit, asked the Episcopal Diocese for permission to use the little church. Farrell, his parishioners, and Jenkins residents renovated the building. It helped that Farrell did electrical work on the side.

In 1969, East Greenwich Boy Scout Troop 59, introduced to the chapel during a camping trip near Batsto, did some repairs.

"They tore out plaster, put in insulation, and put up dry wall, all in one day," according to a Scout official at the time.

Hagaman became pastor in 1970; a group from the Weekstown church formed a board of trustees and leased the Jenkins property from the Episcopal Diocese, eventually buying the church in 1987. Despite its Methodist sponsorship, Jenkins Chapel is nondenominational.

The Sunday service attendance is never more than half a dozen people, but the Methodist Church has kept the little chapel in the pines open.

A fund was started in memory of former Jenkins resident Earl Brown; the donors' names are on plaques at either end of the altar railing. A couple from the Camden area gave money for storm windows; their church donated chairs. A youth group from Willow Grove raised money for the attendance and song boards and collection plate. Someone else donated the cross. A Northfield woman donated an old organ, later replaced by an organ from a Chatsworth church. More money was collected from the little bank Hagaman had made in the shape of a church and placed on the front counter of Mick's Canoe Rentals down the road.

The baptismal font wasn't replaced. It had disappeared, probably stolen.

Hagaman, who grew up in Weekstown, holds summer services in two nearby campgrounds—Wading Pines and Bellhaven. And he spends Sundays visiting local families.

"For the few people that are here, we keep busy," he says.

The Methodist Church also has provided help to needy Jenkins residents.

"When we first came here, things were rough for some of the folks financially," Hagaman explains. "We provided gift certificates at Christmas. We still do."

The chapel had been left unlocked during the week so passers-by could

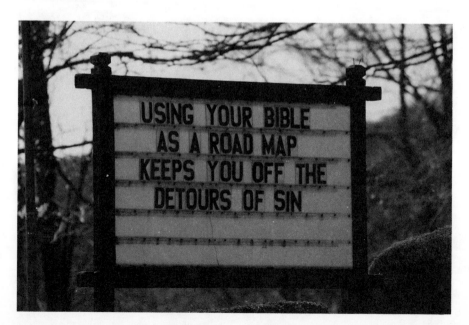

West Milford Calvary Bible Church, Route 513

Wildwood

stop in, but after items were stolen from other churches nearby, the chapel was kept locked. Nevertheless, it is difficult to imagine a more peaceful place to worship than the tiny chapel, especially on a day when the air is fragrant with pine scent and the sun is streaming through the trees.

"Numbers don't count," Hagaman says of the chapel's sparse attendance. "It serves its purpose where it's at. People can come in and sit down and be quiet, if that's all they want."

Troop 59 left its mark on Jenkins Chapel in another way. Assistant Scoutmaster James Denelsback wrote a poem about the church; it is framed on the wall. It ends:

> So if you're near to Jenkins Town
> When Sunday morning rolls around
> Just come right in and set you down
> And see what peace here can be found
> A man can come and lose his fear
> That marks his face with worry lines
> You'll find that love and God is here
> In this small chapel in the pines

*Clinton Hills Baptist Church,
Morris Avenue, Union*

Irvington

Route 547, Lakewood

Newton

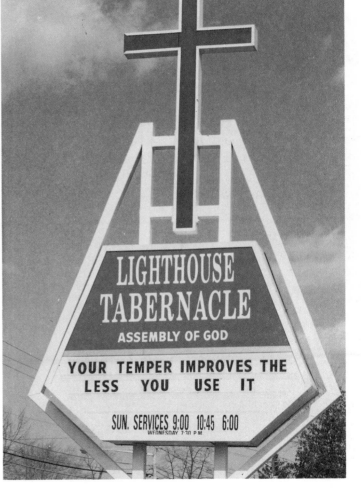

Off Route 38, Mount Holly

Clinton Avenue, Trenton

Ocean Grove

Springfield Avenue, Newark

Calvary Hill Baptist Church,
Route 322, Glassboro

Route 542, New Gretna

*St. John's Lutheran Church, Route
322 eastbound, Williamstown*

Calhoun Street, Trenton

Wild West City, Route 607, Byram

THE DOOR 2 LIFE

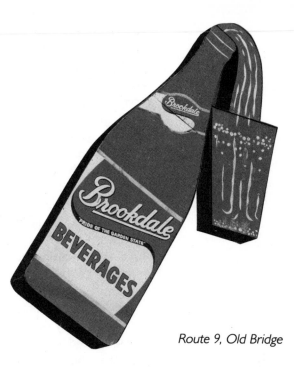

Route 9, Old Bridge

 ew Jersey's roadside art can be found anywhere: on the side of buildings and up on the roof; on billboards, signs, and mailboxes; in the form of paintings, drawings, or sculpture; in something as simple as "I Love You" scrawled on a bridge trestle or as elaborate as a mural painted on the wall of a movie theater.

Two of my favorite examples of roadside art are not easy to find, but they are worth the effort.

On Route 640 in Hammonton, there is a junkyard. But calling EL&M Automotive a junkyard is like calling the Taj Mahal a nice place. This is junkyard as Hollywood production, as circus sideshow. You walk under an archway of orange wheels, past cars, and pieces of cars, and come upon an awesome scene: fifty-five-gallon drums, thousands of them, stretching to the horizon. They are jammed with auto parts: 600 engines, 1,000 transmissions, scores of steering wheels, regulators, alternators, distributors, gears, rod arms—177 different car components in all. Kept in drums to keep them dry, every single part computerized and tagged for easy identification and removal.

"It's a living, breathing thing," says owner Allen Rosenberg, the wisecracking ruler of this twenty-five–employee auto parts kingdom, whose conference room features the grille of a 1970 pink Pontiac protruding from the wall, a glass table resting on two tons of compacted car, and a painting showing his junkyard at the end of a rainbow.

But all this is not what makes EL&M unusual. There are creatures loose in the yard, bizarre-looking things with headlights for eyes, truck housings for legs, and forklift wheels for feet. There is an enormous junkyard dog with tractor treads for teeth and leaf springs for ribs; an "arm" sticks out of its mouth. There is a big turkey by the door with fan blades for tailfeathers. Out in the parking lot is an odd fellow, his gear-and-rod arms holding his housing face as if he has a major headache.

None of the creatures is real, just products of Bill Clark's fervid imagination.

"It surprises people I can look at a pile of junk and see something they don't ordinarily see," says Clark, wearing a cowboy hat and leather jacket.

He visited the junkyard as a kid with his dad, who was not only a preacher but the owner of a garage. There, Clark started "fooling around," making things—primitive robots, rod-stick men. Rosenberg heard about him, and the two struck up a relationship. With such an enormous inventory on hand, Clark was on his way.

"Things," Rosenberg says of Clark's initial creations, "started getting arms and legs."

"Response from people was outrageous," the sculptor/mechanic says. "This one [art] show, I took second place. I thought, 'I can't compete with these people; they're from all over the country.'"

Sylvester Stallone, through a representative, asked Clark to do a Rambo-like figure, but Clark said he had to abandon the project because there wasn't enough time to do it right.

He finds parts at junkyards and flea markets, working on several projects at once because he can't always find the right parts to complete a piece.

"It took me so long to find all those fan blades," he says of his turkey.

*One of Bill Clark's bigger creations,
on Route 54 in Buena Vista*

Think you've got a headache? I've been stuck with this stupid old head for months.
EL&M Automotive, Route 640, Hammonton

"Something like that might take me two months."

His creations are not only around the junkyard but inside the office. A lampshade is made of antique wrenches; a goggle-eyed figure atop an end table holds an ashtray in one hand. Many have funny hats, heads, or hairdos; timing chains can be turned into braids.

"These gears come off motorcycles," says Clark, pulling a foot-high sculpture off a shelf. "They're hard to find because people reuse them."

Considering the enormousness of Rosenberg's junkyard, it's surprising-ing Clark has to look anywhere else for parts.

"I got into the business as a result of not having an education," says Rosenberg, who was earning $125 a week at a repair shop when he bought the junkyard in 1975.

"Actually, I inherited several million dollars and I needed a safe place to keep it," he says, giving the alternate version of the story.

The truth?

"He [the previous owner] said, 'You can't have it, you ain't got no money, you ain't got no education, you can't speak English.' But nobody else wanted it."

Rosenberg scraped up a "few dollars" and bought the yard, removed all the bedsprings, refrigerators, and other junk, put up a stockade fence, and started turning EL&M into a recycling industry showcase. Photos of the yard in 1975 are captioned "The Lemon." By 1978, "The Lemon" had become "The Lemonade Stand."

"We sell virtually every part that comes from the car, like the farmer that sells the oink from the pig," says Rosenberg.

He and Clark—Jewish junkyard owner, black artist—make an interesting pair. In the not-about-to-be-released-anytime-soon movie about EL&M, Rosenberg sees himself being played by Richard Dreyfuss, his wife by Bette Midler.

The biggest sculpture Clark has done was an eighteen-foot-high robotlike figure for a Newark junkyard. His favorite piece, though, was a gear man he fastened on the trunk of his car. It would, by means of a cable in its arm, shoot water at startled motorists.

"That," Clark says, "was the best toy I ever had."

He once made a dog from springs; one touch would set its tail wagging for ten minutes.

ROADSIDE NEW JERSEY

The sculptor's dream: to open up a shop on Route 322 in nearby Cecil to display and sell his work. In the meantime, anyone wishing to see what can be made from pipes, rods, fanbelts, and other auto parts should stop at the Technicolor junkyard on Route 640, right off Route 30.

"Lot of people say they mistook it for an amusement park," Rosenberg says. "That pleases me to no end."

The atmosphere inside the room in downtown Paterson is not festive, but the kids—Arlene, Huhscar, Valerie, Alexia, Santos, and the others— are making the most of it. It is the next-to-last day of the program that has brought them to the basement room on Main Avenue every weekday for the past year.

The program, Next Step, sought to educate "at-risk minority and

The mural painted by the Next Step kids on the wall of the Father English Multi-Purpose Community Center in downtown Paterson

runaway and homeless" eleven- to eighteen-year-olds about drug and alcohol abuse—and the world around them. Speakers came in to talk about everything from narcotics to nutrition. There were group discussions, recreational activities, field trips to Sandy Hook, Seaside, and Suntan Lake.

"As long as the program runs, the kids will be off the streets," says Laura Erickson, Next Step's director of counseling services.

But federal funding wasn't renewed, so the program ended. But Next Step lives on, in a vivid mural on one side of the Father English Multi-Purpose Community Center. There are flowers everywhere, scenes of the Great Falls and downtown Paterson, several love notes and peace signs. Written on a door at the far end of the wall is this message: The Door 2 Life.

"We knew we wanted to put the waterfalls in, we knew we wanted to put Father English in. Other than that, we had no direction," says Next Step art teacher Lori Snack.

Spontaneity carried the day, and a day was all the kids—Tameka Sanders, Beulah Williams, Shawntae McGill, Huhscar Sine, Abraham Dias, Juan DeJesus—plus Snack, assistant Maria Ortega, and recreation director Kent Lawrence needed. The girls gathered at one end of the wall, the boys at the other—"it wasn't planned that way," Snack says—and covered it with messages that speak of hope.

Next Step was one of several programs at Father English, named for the Reverend Francis English, killed in a robbery attempt in the rectory twenty years ago. Other programs include A Child's World/El Mundo del Niño, a day-care program; A Child's Time/El Tiempo del Niño, an all-day kindergarten; an emergency food and assistance program; and Project Youth Haven, a shelter for homeless, runaway, and abused youths, housed in the former convent. All are still in operation.

"They get upset when they can't come here," Erickson says of Next Step. "If they're punished at home and can't come, they call up crying, 'Please tell my parents to let me come.'"

Erickson was hired as a therapist for Next Step, but found herself "doing a lot of legwork for parents who got lost in the system. I would go to court or go to the board of education. Parents would bring me letters from the welfare department that I'd translate for them. Kind of help them help themselves."

A mural was a good opportunity for Snack's art students to show their talent, and the wall needed a makeover in the worst way.

"It was very weird-looking—school buses, stick figures," Snack says of a previous mural the kids painted over. "It wasn't very alive, it was not visually stimulating."

On the next-to-last day of the program, Erickson gathered the Next Step kids in a circle and asked them about the future—theirs and the world's.

"You're going to push a button to send a kid to school," one girl said. "You're going to live like the Jetsons, just you watch."

Erickson then asked what they wanted to be when they grew up.

One girl said a lawyer, another a secretary, a third a singer, a fourth a teacher. One boy wanted to be a professional basketball player, another had it all planned out: "I'll be a millionaire, be married, have a mansion, have a Batmobile."

There are no such fantasies in the mural, which makes up in life and warmth what it lacks in professionalism.

A mural painted on the wall of the Point 4 Theater in Somers Point

Route 33, Wall

The Door 2 Life, drawn on a battered back door, was Kent Lawrence's idea.

"Once you enter a door, all opportunity is there," the counselor-musician says. "People say, 'You've got to give me the key.' You've got to make the key yourself."

"They were singing and crying," Erickson says of the program's last day. "The boys were sobbing. The girls were trying to console them."

"Maybe what we've done will help them move on," she adds. "If some of it sticks, then I'm happy. If only one or two kids is saved from drugs or getting pregnant early, then I'll consider it successful."

The program is gone, but Next Step lives on in the flowers, peace symbols, and love notes splashed across a wall in downtown Paterson.

Route 56, Deerfield

Route 35, Holmdel

Hoboken

Ocean Drive, Lower Township

Hoboken

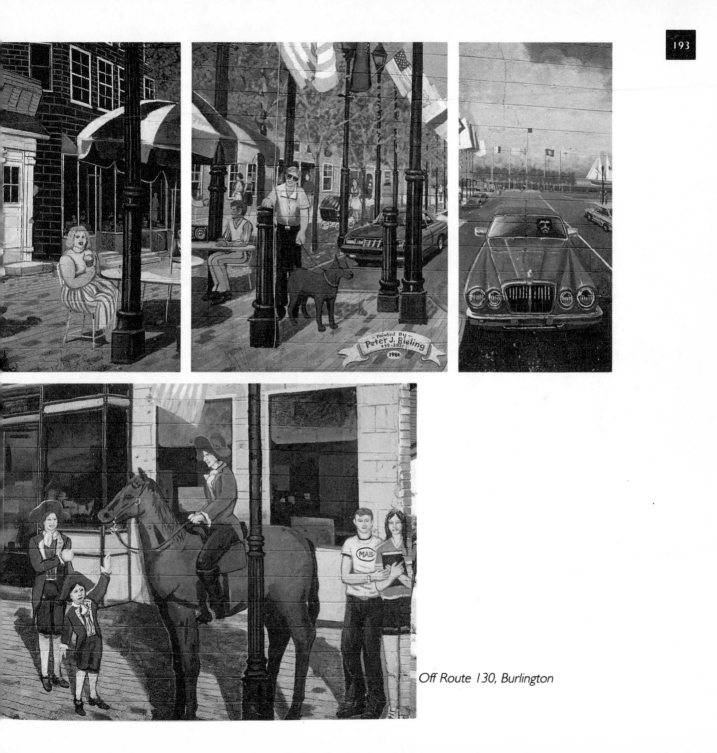

Off Route 130, Burlington

Seaside Heights

Route 57, Franklin, Warren County

Brunswick Avenue, Trenton

The Pipeline, Newark

Route 57, Broadway

Union

West Milford-Ringwood, Passaic County

Route 130, Florence

Route 45, Woodbury

Route 511, Bloomingdale

Asbury Park

Route 46, Lodi

Route 47, Green Creek

Route 1, Lawrence

EPILOGUE

"The World's First Automobile Theater" opened in Camden in 1933. In their heyday—the late 1950s, early 1960s—there were more than four thousand drive-ins across the U.S. New Jersey's last drive-in, the Route 35 Drive-In in Hazlet, closed in 1991. The only reminder of the golden days are the dozens of crumbling drive-in signs around the state.

Route 47

Route 94/206, Newton

Route 77, Bridgeton

Route 33, Wall

Olden Avenue, Ewing

Route 30, Mullica

ABOUT THE AUTHOR

eter Genovese has probably seen more of New Jersey than anyone, having traveled hundreds of thousands of miles around the state in the past dozen years in search of people and places for his column, "Passing By," in *The Home News* of New Brunswick. He lives in Manasquan.